Praise for

STATE
of
EMERGENCY

"A powerful voice in consistently reminding us that we all have a stake in the fight for a just, fair, and equitable America."
—Jada Pinkett Smith,
actor, producer, and entrepreneur

"A masterful book . . . reaffirms the urgency of the current state of Black people in America and the power we all have to win transformative change."
—Marc Lamont Hill,
New York Times bestselling author

"Gives us the words and tools to fight for the justice our families deserve."
—Tamika Palmer,
r of Breonna Taylor

T0108780

"An urgent call for racial justice that demands attention, discussion, and action."

—*Kirkus Reviews* (starred review)

"Shifting between outrage, hope, and resolute determination, this call to action will resonate with readers already fighting for racial justice, as well as those looking to join the movement."

—*Publishers Weekly*

"Mallory gives readers the tools they need to fight injustice and find a pathway towards true freedom."

—*Marie Claire*

"Mallory provides a history of racism in the US, as well as equity-centered pathways forward."

—*Ms. Magazine*

BLACK
PRIVILEGE
PUBLISHING

ATRIA

STATE

of

EMERGENCY

How We Win in
the Country We Built

TAMIKA D. MALLORY

AS TOLD TO ASHLEY A. COLEMAN

BLACK PRIVILEGE
PUBLISHING

ATRIA

New York London Toronto Sydney New Delhi

**BLACK
PRIVILEGE**
PUBLISHING

ATRIA

An Imprint of Simon & Schuster, Inc.
1230 Avenue of the Americas
New York, NY 10020

Copyright © 2021 by Tamika Mallory

First Black Privilege Publishing/Atria Books paperback edition May 2022

BLACK PRIVILEGE PUBLISHING / ATRIA PAPERBACK and colophon are
trademarks of Simon & Schuster, Inc.

For information about special discounts for bulk purchases, please
contact Simon & Schuster Special Sales at 1-866-506-1949 or
business@simonandschuster.com.

The Simon & Schuster Speakers Bureau can bring authors to your
live event. For more information or to book an event, contact the
Simon & Schuster Speakers Bureau at 1-866-248-3049 or visit our
website at www.simonspeakers.com.

Interior design by Tim Shaner, NightandDayDesign.biz

Manufactured in the United States of America

1 3 5 7 9 10 8 6 4 2

Library of Congress Cataloging-in-Publication Data is available.

ISBN 978-1-9821-7346-3

ISBN 978-1-9821-7347-0 (pbk)

ISBN 978-1-9821-7348-7 (ebook)

To my love, to my heart, to my purpose, my son, Tarique.
I know the pain that my work has caused you.
To be present for the world requires my absence
in your life at times when I am needed most.
Know that, while my work takes me to places you
can't follow, you are always with me.
It is because of you that I fight this fight,
to make the world better for you. I see your greatness.
Thank you for being my son and my best friend.

CONTENTS

In order to see where we are going,
we not only must remember where we have been,
but we must *understand* where we have been.

—ELLA BAKER

"Is there room for someone like me?"

I'm from the bottom. To a lot of you reading, you have no idea what that means. The bottom is a place where you have to learn to survive before you get to live. I grew up in the Bronx. That was my bottom, but the bottom applies to any ghetto in America. The faces may change, but the problems in every hood are the same. The bottom is a place where mothers have to figure out how to feed their kids. It's a place where there are no jobs. It's where there are more bodegas and liquor stores than grocery stores. It's where violence is so out of control that you have to slick your face down with Vaseline in case someone tries to fight you on the way to school. It's like a piece of society that America has forgotten, like a piece of a garden that's gone without water, so the only thing growing out the hood is weeds and that unlikely flower that survives through cracked concrete. I guess I would be considered the rose that grew from concrete. I made it out, but a lot of people I love are still there. Still suffering. Still neglected. Nobody can hear their cries for help. So, I use my voice.

Don't get me wrong. I ain't no activist. Tamika is the activist. She's the one the people need. I'm just a real-ass bitch who's not afraid to speak up when I see something wrong. That's the thing that gets me. America is blatant when it comes to disrespecting and systemically murdering people of color. It's obvious. It's wrong, but everybody is afraid to speak up. They're afraid to lose their endorsement deals, afraid to offend their fans, but I can't help it. If I see it, I have to speak it, because I've been blessed with a platform that people pay attention to. Yes, I'm a rapper. Yes, I twerk. No, I'm not trying to be your children's role model. But I still have an opinion on the injustices of Black and brown people. I don't care that I'm not perfect. I don't care that it doesn't come out eloquently. People misunderstand my message sometimes because it comes out wrong. I don't express it like a scholar. I get emotional. I let my anger bring out the accent, and sometimes it exposes the things I don't know. I curse. I call people out. I say all the right things the wrong way, but I'll tell you this—you don't have to be a college graduate to be on the right side of history. My heart leads me to speak up. I don't gain anything from speaking up, for standing with Tamika, for aligning myself with Breonna Taylor's family or bringing awareness to our brothers and sisters locked up in prisons. I just want change. I'm trying to contribute to change. This conversation is for everybody. Every voice belongs at the table. From those surviving at the bottom, like I was once upon a time in the Bronx, to the rich white celebrities who grew up in Beverly Hills. Everyone who is willing to speak about the injustices against people of color should be welcome to this fight. No, I'm not on the front lines. We have our superheroes for that. That's Tamika's place. That's not my place, but the awareness that I can bring with a single tweet, with a single social media post, with a single sound bite, is what I'm bringing to the potluck. That's my contribution, and yes, sometimes I put my foot in my mouth, sometimes I feel out of place, sometimes I feel unwelcome because I'm not a traditional activist, but I still activate.

I hope this book, written by a woman who I look up to, a woman who shows all sides of herself to make sure she is relatable to regular people like me . . . I hope I learn from her words. I hope this book gives me knowledge and helps me understand the history of the plight of people of color. I don't want to study it the way I did when I was in school. I want to feel Tamika's perspective. I want to be inspired and guided to be a better activist so that I use my voice in a way that is impactful to the fight for freedom because I am criticized a lot for speaking up and saying the wrong things. I see people talk about my lyrics and me twerking like those things don't allow me to give myself to injustice. The world makes me feel like I don't have a seat at the table sometimes, but the ones who love to criticize shouldn't care about who is sitting at the table. Whether it's an old-school activist from the great civil rights era or a new-school social media activist. We all want the same things. If I'm doing something wrong in the way I represent the movement, don't shun me, teach me. Help me. Tell me how to use my influence in a way that pushes forward the agenda for justice and equal rights. That's what I want. I'm so honored to be in this book with Dr. Angela Davis. She is our hero. Sometimes because of the haters, I feel like I should just shut up, but I know I can't. It's too serious. Dr. Davis, please tell me and people like me, how do we activate? Are we welcome? How does someone like me, someone who has no political background, who's a little loud, a little unbuttoned, how does that girl or boy from the bottom do their part?

—CARDI B

Foreword
Dearest Cardi B

This pursuit of Black freedom for Black people has persevered over so many centuries and has claimed untold numbers of proponents. I consider myself one of many who have helped to push forward this struggle. It goes without saying that what is necessary to guarantee its continued presence is young people who can guarantee its future trajectory. Yes, of course you are welcome and you know that you are especially needed at this moment. Just as this movement requires the sturdy shoulders, forceful words, and steady leadership of our sister Tamika, we also need your vision, your creative power, and your unabashed political interventions. You inspire Tamika—and you inspire all of us. Young activists today recognize that structures have to be transformed, systems must be changed, and that we need a revolutionary approach to racism, misogyny, climate change, homophobia, and transphobia.

I was eleven years old when the Montgomery Bus Boycott took place and when the southern movement for Black freedom took shape. I have always been critical of the way we are urged to think of this vast freedom movement as only focused on civil rights, which is often narrowly defined as assimilation into the existing order. I advocated for the Black liberation movement because I knew that civil rights was necessary but not sufficient. Even Dr. Martin Luther King, Jr., recognized that Black citizens required more than civil rights. We need justice: racial justice, economic justice, gender justice, and all of the substantive changes that will uplift our communities. As Black people who have historically benefited from the support of indigenous people in slave uprisings and in the creation of maroon communities, we should always be willing to stand with our native sisters and brothers. Our destiny is connected to Latinx struggles. The border must not be the site of racist violence. Nor should we accept racist violence in Occupied Palestine. This is the intersectionality of our struggles.

Black liberation is a pivotal ingredient of planetary justice and all those who imagine emancipatory futures are welcomed at the table. Your affirmation of this movement and of Tamika's role in it demonstrates your commitment to equality. It is important that you and people like you, our artists, cultural workers, and influencers of new generations, are present because you invite critical engagement with our current issues. You all have an important role to play during this period. So many Black youth would not have been politicized if it were not for music culture and especially hip-hop culture. Hip-hop, like everything else, is diverse and full of internal contradictions, but it is absolutely clear that this music has helped to create new communities of struggle. We should not assume that political leaders and scholar/activists are always the ones who have the answers. Most often it is the forgers of our popular musical and visual cultures who know how to invite the world to experience, at the level of feeling, desires for habitable futures that scholars have not figured out how to convey.

I appreciate your humility, Cardi. While "modesty" is not a descriptor that most people would associate with you, the very fact that you are modestly questioning where you belong in this struggle indicates that you are precisely the kind of person we need. Your reluctance to acknowledge yourself as a powerful force for the movement reminds me of the way Nina Simone underestimated the way her art played an essential role in the fight for Black liberation.

Many decades ago, Nina came to visit me while I was in jail. It was a major highlight of the period of my incarceration. As she sat in my cell (I was in a small holding facility in Palo Alto with no visiting room), we discussed Black struggles unfolding at the time. My lawyers had demanded that I have access to any books I needed, so I had a few hundred books stacked against the wall. Nina took a look at the books and commented that she felt like she didn't know anything at all and that she needed to educate herself in order to better participate in the Black movement. I was shocked because I looked up to Nina Simone as one of our leaders in the same way I looked up to other cultural figures like James Baldwin and Harry Belafonte. When Huey Newton's birthday was celebrated by thousands of people at the Los Angeles Coliseum less than two months before the assassination of Dr. King, Nina Simone was the most powerful voice and the only woman on the program that evening. I felt compelled to tell her that she already had more knowledge than most of us, knowledge that moved, inspired, and persuaded people to join the struggle. Her "Mississippi Goddam" probably brought more people to the movement than speeches and political tracts from acknowledged movement leaders. So yes, Cardi, you are welcome: your art, your platform, your heart, your rage, are all welcome. You are an amazing cultural activist and you help to expand the collective movement to achieve justice for those who live under the weight of racism and heteropatriarchy.

There was a time when Black liberation was fundamentally about the liberation of the Black man. This was the approach that most of us took, even women, during the early period of the 1960s. So, this is an exciting moment because not only are we witnessing new ways of standing up against racism, but also ways in which the patriarchal traditions of leadership are falling away. This of course requires us to think about issues of gender and the ways in which binary conceptions of gender have prevented us from recognizing and taking advantage of the full power of possibilities of struggle. If we once thought freedom was freedom for the Black man and we had to argue that women needed to be included in that conception of free-dom, we now recognize that we can't hold on to these anachro-nistic notions. We live in a time where yes, Cardi B, you can be a leader. A woman. A rapper. And you can still speak up when you see injustice. It is important to give women like you the microphone to speak truth to the power of their experiences with injustice. It is equally important to welcome all progres-sive activists, however they express their activism, and espe-cially trans women of color. If we learn how to challenge the binary structure of gender, that means we can also challenge a whole range of racist ideas and structures that have been with us for so long that they appear to be normal.

We are fighting for justice, equality, and for the radical transformation of the conditions surrounding our existence.

We deny ourselves the beauty and the power of collec-tive movements when we assume that all of the participants are required to think and act in the same way. My own defi-nition of activism is always very broad. It does not prescribe how people must think, how they must formulate their ideas, or how they must practice their resistance. It is not limited to certain walks of life and it emphasizes intellectual approaches that emanate from lived experiences and aesthetic awareness as well as from institutionalized learning. Its goal is to build communities and to bring ever larger numbers of people into the circle of radical struggle. Cardi, you can do that with your art, with your music, and with your words. You are just as welcome as those, like Tamika, whom I first met at the 2017

Women's March, who take the podium and inspire us with their forceful speeches.

Many years ago, I came to understand the crucial importance of music and poetry when I visited the island of Grenada in the aftermath of their revolution. I realized that at their rallies the necessary political speeches would occupy no more than 20 to 30 percent of the program, because it was the music and the poetry that the people in attendance really wanted to hear. Art moves people, it educates people, it educates their imagination. So dear, please pull your seat up to this table, take your seat next to Tamika as she offers this book to the world, and be confident that you absolutely deserve that place. So don't be reticent. This is a message to you and to all those who question their own roles in continuing a collective struggle that has been kept alive across generations. We urgently need your name, your voice, your art, your fans. Ring the alarms of justice because we have lived in a state of emergency for far too long. A radical revolution is on the horizon and it is the "unbuttoned activist," in your words, who can relate to the people. We all want the same thing. Change will never come without the collective of organized communities of struggle.

This book—the powerful voice of a generation—offers us glimpses of the history of Black oppression and a guide for those who want to revolutionize our visions of the future. Remember that fearless young woman who gave us the words we needed when we were seeking to express our collective agony in the aftermath of the racist police murders of George

Floyd and Breonna Taylor. Tamika D. Mallory now offers us a radical manifesto that will help to shape future generations of revolutionary freedom fighters. Take heed and move forward.

—ANGELA Y. DAVIS

Prologue
January 6, 2021
Washington, DC

When I think of the most terrifying tools of hatred in this country's history, I don't think of a knife, or a gun. I think of a noose. I think of the Black men and boys whose necks were snapped under the weight of their swinging bodies as they hung from trees. It was paralyzing to see a noose hang in front of the United States Capitol while domestic terrorists breached the complex our congressional leaders use to write our laws. The images of January 6, 2021 left me stunned. The MAGA hats, the rioters scaling the walls of our nation's Capitol, the uncontrollable mob causing destruction and accosting armed police officers without consequence. I took it all in, but it was the sight of the noose that left my chest hollow. The entitlement and privilege that so many still deny even exists was on full display for the world to witness on that day.

Over one hundred years ago, Ida B. Wells took a stance against lynching with her work, her words, and a printing press. She found that the lynchings rampant around the United

States were not the consequence to crimes committed by Black men, as many wished them to be portrayed. Wells found those lynchings to be tools applied to enforce white superiority. The works of white mobs who wanted to keep Blacks in their place, economically and socially.

Fast forward one century later to the leader of this nation inciting the descendants of those mobs to the Capitol with the intent to intimidate, harm, and even murder political leaders. They came with their nooses, the symbol for injustice and murder, to remind Black people to stay in our place. Only these men and women didn't hide behind white hoods. They didn't keep in the shadows. They were emboldened enough to storm a building that hadn't been breached in two hundred years to spit in the face of American democracy.

They were there to protest a new President Biden, and they were there in protest of Vice President Kamala Harris. Because how dare a Black woman be elected to represent a country they feel is theirs to keep. To own. So, they came, nooses hung high to put us in our places.

The infection that sickens America is racism, and the election of our new administration was the lance that forced that sickness out for the time being. Those men and women, unremarkable by appearance but terrorists all the same, came from behind stethoscopes, from behind desks, from behind their suburban gates. We have names. We have faces. Those were cops, they were military men and women, they were Olympians, they were even politicians themselves, attacking their own kind. In case we had forgotten in our moments of relief, this insurrection showed us that racism continues to live around us.

The irony that it took Eugene Goodman, a Black law enforcement officer, to save our nation's congressmen and women from terrorists born and bred to kill their own, shows us what history has shown us time and time again.

Black men, Black people, expected to survive in the most impossible of circumstances, must always persist, expected to sacrifice for the good of "us all" without much recognition expected in return. Eugene Goodman, that Black man, is the epitome of what officers of the law can, should, and must be. He was in immeasurable and imminent danger. He was out-numbered and surely feared for his life, yet he refrained from using deadly force. He didn't fire one bullet. He used his other skills, his training, and his humanity to divert the mob away from their targets of hate and violence. Who is to say what would have happened had he drawn his firearm. Does a bullet stop a mob? Does it fix the hatred in the hearts of man? Would one gun stop dozens or hundreds? Well one man, Eugene Goodman, showed what Black people have wished cops would recognize all along.

That mob showed up to fight. Not for human rights. Not because a member of their community had been shot and killed in her sleep. Not because a member of their community had been murdered by the very people their tax dollars pay to offer protection.

No, they showed up to defend their legacy of oppression

over people of color and to affirm their claim on America as their country and no one else's.

President Biden and Vice President Harris's first days showed some hope. They lifted the bans on Muslim and African people trying to enter this country. They attacked the COVID-19 crisis head-on. But tackling systemic racism is another matter. The attack on the Capitol proved that the issues Black and brown communities have called attention to, marched for, and died for are deep-seated, and the only way to do right by us all is to address this country's history of subjugation.

We can't go forward and unite with our oppressor until that oppressor repents and repairs what centuries of institutional imprisonment, murder, and hatred have wrought. Let's see how the next four years under this administration tackles that. Until they do, this remains a state of emergency.

So, what are we going to do about it?

—TAMIKA D. MALLORY

HOW WE
GOT HERE

One
Our Moment

My book.

That still doesn't feel quite right when I see it. Despite what you may think, I'm not a woman who relishes the spotlight. Especially one cast over me in the wake of destruction. No, I don't like that type of attention at all, so calling this MY BOOK feels self-centered. Calling a book written by a Black woman about race, *mine,* feels small. I come from a long line of Black women who never had the opportunity to put their thoughts to paper for the world to see. We must never forget that literacy is a privilege in this country. The very notion of reading and writing was a crime for my people once upon a time. I come from a lineage of American enslavement where Black men and women were whipped, jailed, and often murdered for attempting to learn to read and write—so it feels selfish to call this *my* book. It's much bigger than that. I see using my voice, my school of activism, my history, and my personal experience to pen a manifesto of freedom as a responsibility to represent every Black man and woman who shed blood in this fight before me. I am my ancestors' wildest manifestation. It is monumental that I'm able to contribute my narrative to history. So no, this isn't *my* book. It belongs to all of us. This is a book about THE MOMENT but also about the people who forged this path to freedom before I was even a thought in my parents' minds. This book is about bringing us—you and me and everyone fed up with the way things have been allowed to be—together to hold our institutions accountable. Finally. For their misuses of power. Their cold-blooded murders. Their pillaging of communities left out and left behind. And this book is a call to action to those who want to do something about it.

It's no secret that America is at war with itself. On a global stage for the world to witness, we've shown ourselves to be at our weakest. In 2020, bias-driven attacks on Black and Asian-Americans pushed reported hate crime to a level last seen in 2008, the year our first Black president Barack Obama was elected. Donald Trump pumped old blood through new veins, reviving a time when overt racism was not only acceptable but expected.

"Systemic oppression" may sound like something trendy and new cooked up by wannabe radicals, but that notion is far from the truth. From the very inception of this nation, the powers that be have brutalized those of different races, religions, cultures, customs, and pigmentations. Starting with the decimation of indigenous American tribes, the founding fathers established this country with a clear hierarchical system in mind. Despite being guests in the New World, Puritans from

2

England claimed to discover a land that was already inhabited. Native people lived in America prior to the false discoveries of Christopher Columbus (and Leif Erikson, too). People were already here. You can't discover what belongs to someone else. The theft and murder that took place upon the arrival of the Europeans was the first act of terrorism on American soil. Native tribes were thriving, growing crops, governing themselves, and enterprising with one another. When the crusade to discover new land brought white men to America, they arrived to loot and conquer that which was not theirs to take. They brought terror and disease. Armed with new technologies of war, a system of enslavement ensued to keep the natives in line. Over 90 percent of that homegrown population was killed off. The land that our leaders—almost all wealthy and white—have the privilege to call free was purchased with the lives of people in all shades of humankind's palette. Whether the currency be by blood or by bondage, ethnic groups outside of Anglo-Saxon heritage paid that hefty price.

Been there and done that, but it needs to be stated again. The greatest unresolved travesty in American history remains the brutal system of human enslavement in the South. It is the origin of Black America. Of impoverished America. Of incarcerated America. Black Americans have faced the most damaging forms of discrimination of any group in this nation's history. While all ethnicities and races have experienced moments of discrimination here, systemic oppression for Black Americans has endured uninterrupted for centuries.

It isn't a moment. It isn't a stretch of time when Black people had it rough and needed to earn their place in line. The invisible knee on the neck of the Black community has never let up. It is the totality of our experience in America, and the clock still ticks, as 402 years of systemic racism precedes me. We were born oppressed, we live oppressed, and we die oppressed. It is a system that offers no reprieve, no reparation, only a recurrence of injustice. It's a cycle. It's a generational burden passed down from the days of enslavement. Doesn't mean there aren't stories of success and Black excellence. Most of our people, however, deal with trauma as a normal part of daily existence.

It has always been in the interest of our oppressors to encourage America's ethnic groups to separate themselves from one another. Tokenized and villainized, Black people have most often been the ones to keep at arm's length. The scapegoats to look down upon as you make your play to move up the social ladder here. But if we look at the treatment of all communities of color over the course of American history, we will realize we are more alike than different. The Black, brown, and immigrant people who built this country's economic infrastructure since the founding of the thirteen colonies have always been welcome only as long as we were useful—and quiet. It's ironic that the Puritans who fled England out of fear of religious persecution went on to settle in the New World and persecute new groups of people they could perceive as below themselves, beginning with the Native Americans. White America has always capitalized off the sweat equity of people of color only to turn around and alienate minorities from the product of that labor. Labor produces wealth. Wealth produces power. Those in power make the laws. And these laws protect the majority and create disparity for every other community. Wealth in the South was accumulated off the beaten backs of African enslaved people. Chinese migrant workers laid down the transcontinental railroad systems that connected east to west. The jobs were so dangerous that there was a shortage of white men willing to do the work, only then opening an opportunity for laborers from the Far East. They carved the railroad through the Sierra Nevada mountains, yet their story is rarely told anymore.

Before them, immigrants from Europe came to nineteenth-century America in droves, attracted by the land of opportunity. What opportunity they could find was often in sweatshops, at manufacturers, and at the mercy of contractors more than ready to exploit their need for employment. Italian, Irish, German, Scandinavian, and Polish workers left home for low wages, poor conditions, and grueling hours. Ellis Island still holds records of the relentless stream of immigrants—all of whom would now be called "white"—who came into America, dispersed throughout the major cities looking for work, and found almost nothing of worth. You see, in America, even white people have seen the face of exploitation. Because here, everything, from enslavement on down to more recent disempowerment of this country's workforce, has always been driven by capitalism and greed.

Green, the color of money, was the motivation behind these unfair systems. America is infamous for its disenfranchisement of communities of color. Our last president put behind bars thousands of immigrants seeking asylum. Guilty of nothing more than seeking refuge, they were locked away in cages while their children were taken and thrown behind barbed-wire fences—or worse. While I am a Black American and I advocate for my community, this prescription for change is necessary for all afflicted communities.

Discrimination and the brutality that stems from it are not only a Black issue. At any given moment, white supremacy can narrow its lens on you. Equality is a shared struggle for marginalized communities, but for Black folks, it has been exceptionally violent and dehumanizing. We've made strides over time, but the Trump era of politics reignited a strain of racism we hoped had been extinguished sixty years ago. Those old stains of blood pushed up through the soil as the rhetoric of white power was pushed forth from the White House. A country that allows the murder and disregard of innocent Black and brown people is a country unworthy of its allies' trust or its citizens' support. Half a decade spent whitewashing this nation, spent denigrating the unique cultures and shades that make this planet the beautiful symphony we know it to be, has left the rest of the world alienated. Black men killed by racist police and gangs—yes, *gangs*—of white-supremacist vigilantes. The president of the free world sent dog whistles clear as day to white supremacists, instructing them to stand by for action. Those same vigilantes stormed the Capitol Building armed with white privilege as protection. If it had been a nonviolent protest for Black freedom and justice, it would have ended tragically, yet these thugs, yes, thugs, were escorted out of the Capitol Building without the exercising of force. I'd bet that not a single body camera malfunctioned that day. We've all woken up some during the past few years and felt like we're in *The Twilight Zone*, a place where everything we accepted as reality was turned upside down. It is a terrifying time to be Black in America. This book is my counterattack on that disorienting feeling.

I step foot in the streets to protest in the pursuit of justice. There are moments along that pursuit that feel lonely. I am not new to activism—this has been a twenty-five-year journey for me, and it has not always come with support and understanding. Many out there perceive me as an angry Black woman. Well, I am. I am angry because Black people are under attack by the very entity we've been told represents safety. I am angry because my community and the communities of my people are policed based on appearance rather than on suspicion. I am angry because innocent, unarmed Americans are being murdered left and right, for no justifiable reason, by the state sworn to protect them. How can you sit by and watch a George Floyd cry out for his deceased mother while being choked out by a racist cop, and feel anything less than anger? "Angry Black woman" is accurate. I've personally never contested that, but recently, others have begun to share in my rage. The world has been awakened to the inherent pain of the Black experience. Whether it be through personal tragedy or through witnessing injustice over social media, there has been an influx of support, an outcry, demanding justice. It's a moment that has been a long time coming. Two hundred and forty-six years in the making, in fact. We cannot abide a world where humanity condones brutality by gun, by cop, by neglect, or by dollars.

We are in the middle of a revolution in America. Not the type of revolution white supremacists are fighting for. This is a revolution about true freedom and equity. We the people are fed up and will not silently stand by any longer. Donald Trump is no martyr, but his deplorable rise and fall exposed cracks we've all needed to see in this project we call the United States of America. He brought out the worst in us, but he also reminded us of the best in us as we pushed back against his poisonous agenda. History books tell you that revolutionaries wear tricorn hats or practice guerilla warfare in battlefields a world away—but they also live on your block, attend your church, teach in your schools, share your ideals, and do their work at home, shedding light on inequities and reminding friends and colleagues of the humanity we *all* share.

More than forty countries around the world joined the protests in 2020 against the brutalization of Black people. We saw an awakening. The entire planet recognized the plight of Black Americans and decided that enough is enough. The world's beacon on a hill can no longer also project violence globally and leave its underclasses to suffer. People are choosing a side. Not everybody, but many.

Racist vs. Anti-racist.
Right vs. Wrong.
Moral vs. Immoral.

We must ask ourselves what type of world we want to live in. What type of society do we want to pass on to our children? If you are new to this fight, racism may not be easily identifiable to you. It is not always obvious, so let me be clear in my definition of what a racist is.

A RACIST individual is someone who believes their race is superior and will lie, kill, or steal to keep and impose that power.

It is not enough to be nonracist. In the words of Ibram X. Kendi, an ANTI-RACIST is someone who believes in equality and recognizes racism and fights against it, even within themselves.[1] All communities come with their ideas of what other communities might be like. Everyone has bias. Everyone makes assumptions. Judgments. It is not realistic for me to say otherwise. It's nice to think of oneself as more enlightened than the rest, but in truth none of us is perfect. We all have moments of prejudice. We all have categorized a group of people based on history and stereotypes imparted long before we ourselves were born. And that is why being nonracist is not enough. We must work hard to go *against* racism. Whether it be institutional or personal, an anti-racist will check racism whenever and wherever it is present. An anti-racist operates at a heightened state of awareness and is aware that skin tone creates unfairness in the world. Anti-racists actively attempt to level the playing field for different communities of people.

The alternative—not making a choice—is still making a choice. We live in a digital world where the excuse of ignorance no longer applies. There is no such thing as "I didn't know." In the past, a Northerner would never encounter the truth of racism that existed in the Jim Crow South. Or you might genuinely have been oblivious to the struggles of people held down in other places around the world, in Palestine or the Sudan. There was a level of concealing racism in the past. Today you know. Today you are aware. In a time when hashtags carry word of injustice around the world with the click of a button, there is no way for you not to know. It is right in front of your eyes, day after day, murder after murder. A lot of people have been asleep during the freedom fight.

Now is the time to wake the hell up.

This Book.

My Book.

Our Book.

The book of the moment rings the alarms of righteousness because humankind is in a state of emergency. My people are dying. Black people are dying.

OUR people are dying.

Two

Legacy of an Activist

WHERE I CAME FROM

I guess I should begin with my name. Tamika D. Mallory. The Mallory name is rooted in activism. I can trace it back as far as 1861. Shepard Mallory, who I believe to be my ancestor, was one of the slaves who helped end Black enslavement for all in America.[1] He was one of three enslaved Black men who decided to defy an order from their master, Colonel Charles Mallory. He caught wind of impending orders to help construct an artillery emplacement for the Confederacy in North Carolina.

Shepard Mallory, along with Frank Baker and James Townsend, fled upon learning of their master's plans. They feared being away from their families. Today it sounds simple to think of someone running away, but it was a weighty decision for men with loved ones still in bondage. Not only did they risk their own lives by fleeing, but the punishment for doing so would likely be passed down to those they left behind.

Still, they took the chance at freedom. Union soldiers from the North were nearby, too close not to take the leap of faith.

Just seeing the name of the family that used to own mine, the master who stripped me of the African surname that was rightfully mine, gives me chills. I'm a Mallory because this white man purchased my ancestors. It's wild to think of yourself as a possession to be bought and sold, but it's a part of who I am. Sorry. That's off topic, but it's what comes to mind when I think of where I came from. I'll try to stay focused.

They took a rowboat across Hampton Roads in Virginia to Fort Monroe. The three of them were seized upon arrival by Major General Benjamin Butler. The Union leadership didn't quite know what to do with the three slaves. The Fugitive Slave Act required that the three men be returned to their owner, but Virginia had just seceded and was a self-governing state, bound only by its own laws, meaning the commander at Fort Monroe wasn't obligated by federal law to return the slaves. The valuable information about the Confederate Army's plans to build more artillery forts made Shepard Mallory and the other men valuable assets at Fort Monroe, but by law, they were not even considered people. They were property, and by the letter of the law, their owner being a Confederate colonel made them contrabands of war. General Butler couldn't return Confederate contraband that could be harmful to his mission. Instead, he offered the men refuge and let them become laborers within Fort Monroe. For some Union soldiers, it was their first time being in the presence of a slave, and through their interactions, they learned that Black people in the South were human beings, just like everybody else they knew. Shepard Mallory's decision to escape to Fort Monroe caused a ripple effect, drawing more enslaved people to Union lines seeking refuge, forcing President Abraham Lincoln to finally address not just the approach to war but the circumstance of enslaved people waiting for the outcome.[2] Those three brave men in bondage, one of whom is my blood ancestor, started a movement that created contraband slaves, building to more than forty thousand freed men and women who made it to Union lines.

That is the type of stock I come from. Bravery in the face of death. Pushing forward when fear tells me to turn back. Sacrificing everything for freedom. Those characteristics were not learned. They were inherited. From Fort Monroe, to my parents in Harlem, New York, who were students of the movement, to me. Going along to get along has never been the behavioral model of my family. Generational activism is a part of carrying the Mallory name. Dinner-table talk in my household coming up consisted of planning action agendas for upcoming rallies and discussions about Blackness, freedom, and equality.

My parents raised me in an environment of social awareness, while at the same time trying to shield me from the decay of the projects by sending me to private schools most of my life. My elementary school was across the street from home, but the discipline and structure made it feel like a different place. Later, the challenge became the discrimination I experienced in school from the administration and teachers. After all, I was still a Black girl.

I lived in the middle of Harlem. Manhattanville projects raised me. I earned my degree from the streets on the corner of 133rd and Old Broadway. Drugs, guns, single-parent households, pickup basketball games, hanging out with my homegirls on the bench, laughing at the neighborhood crackheads (addiction was everywhere). It was all part of the experiences that shaped my childhood. Seeing these things, living among them, becoming numb to violence in proximity, seeing addiction up close, all desensitized me to the abnormality of growing up in those circumstances. My upbringing instilled a resilience that I use to navigate my adult life. I am from that experience. I don't need to do hours upon hours of research to confirm how the system's neglect of its social welfare programs in inner cities led to the deterioration of Black neighborhoods. I saw it with my own eyes. I understand that it is not the people who live in the concrete jungle who make it wild, it is those who built that jungle in the first place. Under-resourced neighborhoods like the one I grew up in foster a sense of desperation. Starve someone long enough, and they will find ways to eat by any means necessary. Survival is human nature. The enterprise of dealing drugs, even the use of them, while detrimental, are a means to an end. The ghettos of America have created generations of people numb to things that would cripple the average person. Drugs are coping mechanisms used to treat the trauma of an experience that is inescapable. Inner-city neighborhoods are surrounded by invisible fences that trap their inhabitants, keeping generations of families stuck in the perpetual underclass of America. Affluent people schedule weekly appointments with their mental health advisers to seek therapy for their traumas. The disenfranchised seek the same help, but access to top-notch therapists and their velvet couches isn't abundant. Where the average person can obtain support services, or even pop a pill to take the edge off their pain, Black and brown people endure until they can't anymore. There is nothing normal about the state of Black America—living beneath the poverty line within this capitalist country, inside redlined communities, and brought up in war zones.

Let me be clear. POVERTY IS VIOLENCE. America must stop pretending that Black and brown youth have the same chances of success as everyone else. How can marginalized children succeed when they are busy figuring out how to survive? I know what some will contest this with: "Black on Black crime." Many think that the violence in the Black community is self-inflicted, but it really isn't. America starves Black and brown communities across America and then puts one piece of bread on the table. What do you think will happen?

The hungry fight over that one piece of bread. They steal for it, they kill for it, they lie for it, because if they don't, they die. That math isn't hard to figure out. It's the lack of resources that creates conflict within the community. It's a desperation with which too many Black people decide they must make a way out of no way, despite the moral compromise required. The crime that plagues disenfranchised communities is there because opportunities to excel are not.

When we send young men and women off to war, the government at least pretends to provide therapy and diagnoses for those who struggle with PTSD afterward. When you're in the ghetto and see your neighbors gunned down on a regular basis, the system offers no sympathy, but the trauma still exists.

I participated in two communities growing up. One of privilege in the private schools that educated me. The other without privilege, where my perspective was shaped on the way the world works. That dance with privilege gave me an early understanding of just how poorly served the Black community is in this country. That was one of the motivations that pushed me to the modern movement for justice. The need to bring change to Harlem and every Black community around the country just like it. The desire for schools with up-to-date technology, books, buildings free of rodents, libraries stocked with resources, grocery shelves full of more produce than boxed junk, and doctors who care, right in the epicenter of those communities most in need of their services.

THE LUCKY ONES

I was one of the lucky ones. I saw how the people lived. I was able to vacation outside of the projects during the year, when my parents created other experiences for our family, and I say that word "vacation" purposefully. I say it because I took a break from the violence, a break from the normalizing of winos, junkies, and gunshots. It was a vacation from the daily perseverance of growing up in the trenches of war. Many of us wear persistence as a badge of honor, but think of the lives, the brilliance, the ideas, the *time* we sacrifice to the struggle.

As a Black child in the hood, you normalize those things because they're all you know. I was fortunate to have parents who understood how important it was to provide me with an escape. I wasn't removed from the struggle, but I did have balance. While we couldn't afford to completely move out of Harlem until I was older, they did everything in their power to give me an outside perspective. It ensured that I would not repeat the cycle of existing, and that I would have instead a chance at living, because there is a difference. The "majority," the direct descendants of the founders of this country, get to live. Every person reading this at this very moment may not fully understand the difference just yet, but I guarantee you there's a whole bunch of Black and brown people who know full well the difference between living and existing.

As the daughter of two activists, I witnessed injustice after injustice at every stage of my upbringing. I didn't learn

17

about the plight of the Black community or the harms of racial capitalism in a sociology class. I was a part of the class of people those sociologists studied. The misunderstood. The impoverished. The disenfranchised. The subclass of citizens that America hates to acknowledge. Growing up in the ghetto is as traumatic as it is empowering. Many can't fathom that, but it's true. There is a pulse on the dilapidated streets of Harlem and, I'm sure, every other ghetto across America. It's a culture. It's a shared experience of survival. If you escape it, you really aren't afraid of anything, because you've already beaten what was designed to destroy you. I was a part of the struggle that mainstream America swept under their rugs. My philosophies aren't secondhand knowledge but degrees I earned from the school of hard knocks. I grew up in one of the world's roughest concrete jungles; during the emergence of the crack epidemic, I was a little Black girl who understood very early that I was looking at life through the bars of a trap designed within a system of white supremacy. I can't remember a time before I was mobilizing against injustice. My parents were active in the pursuit of justice for Black people. As a child, I was a tagalong to and a reluctant participant in freedom rallies every weekend. There were no Saturday-morning rituals of cartoons. I was alongside my parents as they worked in the community. When you're that young, you don't really know what you're a part of, but I was subconsciously soaking up my environment. Learning how to organize, learning commitment, listening to the strides my community was taking as well as the hard losses that it endured as I aged in the background.

DOING NOTHING IS DOING SOMETHING

Maybe most important was learning firsthand that doing nothing is doing something. It is strengthening the neglectful patriarchy built on our foundation of racism. It is unacceptable to be an idle bystander. I'm no poli-sci student who set out with big dreams to change the world. I'm from the bottom. The front line was my classroom, and experience was my teacher. I know firsthand what it looks like when the system fails a community of people because 1980s Harlem was supposed to trap me too. I was set up to be a statistic, but I persevered. I used my street savvy and mixed it with the education I was receiving in private schools, applying the combination as a skill set to navigate social issues and local politics. Not many come to the movement from my area of expertise because my specialization can't be studied. It's personal for me.

When I look back at some of the friends who I once walked side by side with, my heart breaks. We all started in the same place, from the same sandbox. Life has beaten them up. The trap of the ghetto ate them alive—while I took vacations, they had no means to escape. The view outside their dirty project window was filled with images of ambulances and body bags being carried out of buildings, because every other day, somebody else was killed in our neighborhood. It's hard to aspire past that limited view. You can't see past the cracked concrete, the graffiti-tagged walls, or the police tape. Too many of my childhood friends rotted there, and it's not because they were incapable of elevation. They were held back because the door to escape is padlocked from the outside. The key holders, the gatekeepers to wealth, health, and the mere possibility of success, sit in neighborhoods miles away, unmoved by the destruction happening in inner-city urban areas. If you're not a ballplayer that a higher-education institution can exploit for profit on a field or court, it's difficult to find another way out. Even the smartest kids in marginalized environments have chains that keep them there. There is a wealth of ingenuity in the hood. Kids who think outside the box, kids who create, kids who innovate, ones who work their asses off but are never acknowledged, are never seen because they are shining on the wrong stage.

In my early adolescence, I spent my time defying my purpose. Being a teenager in my neighborhood was everything. Harlem was like the mecca of all things cool. It was where hip-hop fashion was birthed, where people remixed high-end threads into custom pieces, and forget real famous folks, we had real live hood celebrities right there in the projects. It was the backdrop to my coming-of-age story, and I was so immersed in the lay of the land that I had no idea the life I was living was dangerous. Looking back, I don't know if it was riveting or completely reckless, but it felt like the top of a roller-coaster ride. I was young, cute, and testing the limits of my freedom to make my own choices. Activism was the last thing on my mind. Most of my thoughts centered around boys. It's funny, because the types of boys I liked then are the same grown men I advocate for now. Society labeled them thugs, but teenage Tamika drew their names in hearts inside my notebook. I did not subscribe to the stereotypes then or now. Society misinterprets the plight of inner-city youth, mistaking frustration with aggression and labeling all Black boys as problematic. They were my peers. They were the ones who bought out the ice-cream trucks for the little kids around the way whenever it came around. They were the boys I watched play pickup basketball games until the streetlights came on. They were familiar, and although some of them were falling through the cracks of the system, they were still my people. Young Tamika wanted to take one of those neighborhood boys and love him forever. I wanted to be wherever the action was. Partying. Drinking. Smoking. At the time it seemed cool, but I know now that there was a lack of alternative programming for kids in the projects. There were no piano lessons, no gymnastics, no art classes. If there were, they were not free, and most people in the projects didn't have money to pay for anything other than bills. Food is sometimes optional, so an extracurricular is laughable. There were no accessible, affordable resources to develop Black youth in the community, so we spent our time . . . wasting time.

Saturday mornings, I was at rallies with my parents, and on Saturday evenings, I was turning up with my friends and chasing boys. I was straddling a fence, with one foot in the streets and one in my parents' world of wokeness. I was messing up. I was headed in the wrong direction, and I resisted everything I knew I was expected to become. It's hard to embrace your destiny when it seems so far away. Teenage Tamika would have laughed if someone had told her that her adulthood would be filled with fighting for marginalized groups and being looked at as the face of a movement. It just wasn't in my trajectory. It wasn't something I pursued or aspired to be. I was a product of the streets in my mind, but my soul was a product of a rebellious ancestry too potent to dilute.

TRAGEDY HITS HOME

The birth of my son, Tarique, saved me. There is a shift that happens when you feel life growing inside you, a power you realize you have, and an instinct to protect what comes from you. Prior to having my son, I felt like I had no one to be accountable to. Motherhood gave me purpose and made me realize that I was living for more than myself. The status quo was good enough when I had no one else to consider, but when I became a mother, I knew I wanted my son's view of the world to stretch even further than what I had seen. If I didn't find a way to break through that locked door that kept us all trapped in the projects, in poverty, living out of buildings that were falling apart, my son would be doomed to repeat that existence. Motherhood made me realize the responsibility and crippling fear that came with caring for a Black male in a white society. I had to anticipate every trap that could end my son's life and then teach him how to identify them and how to avoid them. While other mothers of boys from different communities were teaching their kids how to live, I was teaching mine *how not to die*.

The weight placed on my shoulders the moment my son took his first breath was heavy, and it became my duty to develop a strength bold enough to carry it. I had to do everything in my power to make sure he didn't become another victim of the patriarchy. Another statistic. Another headline. Becoming a mother was a blessing. It's an unconditional love unlike anything else in the world, but it's terrifying to be the mom to a Black boy. It was crippling to know that my son would be villainized and judged at first glance, appearance coming before character. I held unreasonable fears about him playing with toy guns, his choice of clothing, and the way he reacted to authority. They all haunted me because I knew that one wrong move could land my Black son in the grave. Mothers should never have to bury their children, but in this country, Black mothers routinely bury their sons, and often their children's fathers. That became my story on a cold April day in 2001 when Jason Ryans, my son's father, was murdered.

Until recent years, I didn't talk much about what happened to him. There is so much pain tied to the moment that I accepted activism as my fate. Jason was beaten, stabbed, and murdered by a group of people he called friends. He was accused of stealing a safe containing drugs and guns that belonged to two men in the group. After beating and stabbing him, they bound him and then pretended to drive him to a rural hospital. All along, they intended to find a secluded spot to murder him. He was shot twice, once in the head and once in the chest, and pushed off a cliff. I remember being in a car when I got the news. My mom called, but she was afraid to tell me while I was out. She wanted me to come home because she had something important to say, but I heard the distress in her voice. I knew something was wrong. My last suspicion was Jason being killed. At first I thought something was wrong with Tarique. My motherly instinct was going haywire, and I refused to hang up the phone until she told me what was going on. His murder stopped my entire world from spinning. I remember my homeboy Kevin and I pulled over on the side of the road, and I immediately thought about my son and how he would never know his father. He had just turned two years old.

There are certain moments in life that change you. They just rip up the foundation of everything you think you know. Everything you think you are. They change the smell of the air, the taste of your favorite food, the beat of your heart. This death disrupted my entire existence, giving me a pain that would later transform to purpose. When Jason was killed, I had to do something with that energy, because if I allowed it to fester, it would consume me. I had to find understanding, because my main question was why? Why did this happen?

But when I removed my emotions and began to look at the situation from a broader lens, I began to see that I wasn't the only one grieving. My son wasn't the only fatherless child in my community. I had seen this story play out time and time again. Funerals were more common than weddings in the projects. When you're that close to death, it doesn't even garner a reaction when it isn't someone who directly affects you. You put it on top of the pile of bad things that happen in the hood and you keep going. I didn't see the issue with gun violence in my community until it hit close to home. The problem is magnified when it happens to you. The search for the why of it all had been in front of my face my entire childhood.

There were a lot of different failures within the framework of the hood that led to that moment. It was not only inevitable, in Jason's case, but likely to happen again to another Black man. It took personal tragedy for me to begin to connect the dots between the violence in my community and the violence of the system around that community. I finally began to question how the environment and decisions made about withholding resources from that environment stimulate the behaviors of those who lived there. White people looking at Black problems, judging from the outside, thinking my son's father's death didn't count because he wasn't living right, can't understand why I blame the system for his death. If you're not from a Black, underserved community, you can't possibly relate to the circumstances that contribute to young Black boys and men getting mixed up in drugs and violence.

Jason was never able to plant his feet firmly on the ground. His entire life was about survival. While he had the most amazing grandparents who he lived with, who attempted to fill the shoes of his parents, it just wasn't the same. They did everything they could to help him, but no matter how hard they tried, it just wasn't enough to save him. There are those who are able to focus on the love they were raised with, and then there are those who have to focus on survival. The survivors are the people who struggle for every little thing, things most of us take for granted, like lights and heat and food and shelter: the people with no one to ask for help and with nothing to lose. It wasn't that Jason didn't have a family, but the family unit he needed wasn't there, and these circumstances pushed him into making bad decisions. He wasn't thinking of the damage that drugs caused his own family, and yet he participated in the destruction. Jason's family had done everything they could, but his inner struggle had a hold on his life. In the last few months prior to his murder, he was homeless, and many days he was thinking about putting a meal in his starving belly. He was sleeping on the floor of an abandoned apartment building. He would hang out all day at the houses of friends, pretending to be okay, when in the back of his mind he knew he didn't have a place to go at night. Can you imagine living under those conditions? Not even having a safe place to take your children? Trying to hide from the world the fact that you are homeless? Desperation put him on a deadly path, and it's not an excuse—it's just the reality of his plight. His parents weren't around. They weren't options for additional support. As is true for too many children of underserved communities in America.

LIFE WITH NO SAFETY NET

Black American children are overwhelmingly raised in unstable environments or in foster care:[3] 61.3 percent of Black children are raised in single-parent households, compared to just 25.7 percent of white children's households.[4] But despite the struggles and the stereotypes, Black fathers actually spend more time with their children than those of other races.[5] Black fathers often try hard to be good dads, but poverty and the system get in the way.[6] We also need to acknowledge that Black families, stretched thin without generations of accumulated wealth to draw on, also rely on extended family and kinship networks that do not always look like the Western nuclear-family structure. All thanks to cycles of poverty, incarceration, illness, and premature death shaped by centuries of structural racism.[7]

Young men and women in other communities function knowing full well there is almost always a safety net in place to protect them as they mature into adulthood. Other races have a foundation of family that young boys and girls can fall back on should they find themselves in an unsafe predicament. My son's father and many Black youths are left to fend for themselves. The family unit is fractured due to imprisonment, due to welfare programming, due to drug and alcohol abuse. Jason couldn't go back to his childhood residence to pull it together. He couldn't borrow money until he was back on his feet. He couldn't even go home to his parents to get a warm meal. He had to make a home out of an abandoned building until he could figure out his next move. His parents had been in and out of jail a majority of his life. His mother dealt with the sickness of addiction, and her life ended very early. That was the hand he was dealt. The cards were stacked against him from the beginning. Imagine if he had access to acceptable housing. Imagine if, instead of his parents being locked up for their struggles with addiction, they were provided with real treatment programs. Imagine if those addictions had been treated at their root causes—mental illness—before self-medicating with drugs became the most easily accessible option. Imagine if access to mental health programming was available, if jobs were readily available. I ask myself often if my son would have a living father today had these things been in place for Jason. There were so many voids in his life that contributed to his death. If even one of them had been filled, perhaps his story would have ended differently. All the trouble he got into doesn't remove the value of his life. His murder awakened me to the larger issues at hand in the world.

This heartbreak marked the first time I would pause long enough to dissect my life. Was I on the road to becoming the type of woman I wanted to be? The type of mother I wanted for my son? Until that point, I had made some bad decisions.

I was living fast and irresponsibly. People judged my choices. I was a young Black woman from the projects with no sense of direction. Teachers wrote me off for being too mouthy, loud, and hardheaded. Family members and elders in the community saw me rebelling and said I wouldn't amount to anything. Then, when I became a young mother, people discounted me even more. All they saw was a walking statistic. Yet another example of what was wrong with Black America. I learned at a young age that people make assumptions based on what they can see. America has proved time and again there is nothing easier to see, identify, and ostracize than Black skin. The Black community is neglected. Streets are filled with potholes. Abandoned buildings are left to decay. Businesses move out. Grocery stores are nonexistent. Only churches and liquor stores fill the ghetto because the systems that run this country don't see value in the Black community. They don't see anything worth investing in, worth fixing, worth educating, worth growing. They leave it destitute and stand by waiting for it to self-destruct.

THE NUANCES OF THOSE YOU FEAR

The majority of the majority, mainstream white America, sees the surface of Black and brown communities but never learns the nuances that contribute to the full picture. What is available by sight alone is not always the full story. My history was filled with the dichotomy of the struggle in the hood versus the world of privilege I saw when I visited the homes of my parents' upper-class friends from work. I hit the pavement with purpose because I am both a part of the disenfranchised that I'm advocating for and blessed with the knowledge of how movements are made to matter. I'm not sitting high on the mountaintop shouting down at the people, I'm among the people. I *am* the people. I'm far from perfect. I've been dirtied up in these streets. I have the emotional scars to prove it. My darkest moments made me into the woman I am today. They shaped my perspective. They taught me empathy. They keep me humble because I didn't come from the outside with an agenda to fix the broken. I'm broken too, I'm hurt too. I mess up too. When I see Black people being treated with less respect than they deserve, I feel disrespected too, because at any moment of any day, that can be my experience. I'm in this fight not because I want to be but because I must be. This isn't a hobby or an intellectual exercise—I am my brother's keeper, my sister's keeper, and when one is brutalized, we all are injured.

Jason's death was a wake-up call. I had rebelled so much against my parents' teachings that I easily could have been dead right beside him. It was not only about my personal loss, although that weighed heavily on me. It was about every kid from around my block who had been murdered over the years. It was about every R.I.P. that had been printed on a T-shirt, and about every curbside vigil I had attended for a Black boy in my neighborhood.

What put these boys out there on the streets? Why are they out there? Who are they trying to feed? What is their story? Drugs do not make themselves or originate in the ghetto. They come from outside the community, from all over the world. Guns too. We do not own gun factories. We do not grow coca plants. You won't find any commercial-scale marijuana growers in Harlem. Yet these things are all more accessible in Black neighborhoods than anywhere. These tools of self-destruction are put in the hands of young Black men more often than any schoolbooks. Society looks at Black people as percentages. The environment produces numbers. Percentages of murders per capita. Single-parent households. Percentages of children reading below grade level. Percentages of theft.

Numbers. Numbers. Numbers. Those numbers have stories, they have pain, struggle, and a mental burden that comes from being stuck in a position of poverty. Statistics don't reveal the entire truth.

Black America does not begin life at the starting line. We are born into the race already losing, so our first mistake will likely be our last. We are not afforded second chances. It is what happens to all Black boys who find themselves sucked up in the pitfalls of the ghetto. They begin to believe what society tells us from day one, that we aren't worthy of more. Underserved children become underserved adults, only adults learn to feed themselves. When society refuses to build up a community, a misguided person will tap any resource that is readily accessible in order to survive.

I know you're wondering how I can advocate for the people who make the wrong choice. But I see humanity inside everyone living in affliction. I don't look at the problems of the urban communities from the outside. I still see it from the inside. I knew these men who society labeled thugs. They were somebody's son, somebody's father, my son's father. I stand up for them because even when a Black man does everything right in his lifetime, he is still viewed the same. We are all participants in a fixed race.

Three
Justice Is Not a Comfortable Fight

MY CALLING

In my forty years of living, I have never encountered any obstacle more terrifying than raising a Black son, alone, in America. Gun violence dismantled our lives when I was nineteen years old. I was angry. A mixture of grief and confusion made me desperate for change, desperate for answers about how this had become my life.

I began to look at the options available to my son and me. There was no safety net, no contingency plan for the loss we had endured. I questioned everything, and every single answer led me back to the system that was set up for failure. Tragedy reignited those childhood lessons that I had learned at the rallies I would attend. I was called to venture down the paths my ancestors had laid out for me. I was already equipped with the knowledge of how to organize because I had been taught to do it as a child, but the personal motivation—my why—was ignited when grief hit close to home. I wanted to break the system that allowed my community to decay and self-destruct. I wanted to activate, and for the first time in my life, it was by choice that I would engage in a movement to seek change. Though we can't allow them to be our only starting point, grief and trauma help move people to action. My grief moved me to activate.

HISTORIANS WERE MY TEACHERS

Reverend Al Sharpton's National Action Network (NAN) was a huge part of my childhood. My parents were two of the first members of this newly formed civil rights organization, and boy, were they faithful. Every Saturday they attended rallies; that still goes on today in Harlem. The structure of NAN was a lot like church, and my parents were a part of many of the committees. Even when there were no pressing issues to protest, NAN gathered to educate the community about Black culture and to organize for the fight ahead. We would sing, we would commune with one another, while contributing to the struggle for Black liberation. It was a community, and I participated out of habit and necessity for years, even when I didn't recognize the path of activism as my own. It was just in me. I was programmed to be socially conscious, and I contributed in whatever ways I was needed. When we were young, it was the Youth Move movement; as we grew older, I eventually gained major responsibility. I was following the path that my parents saw for their bigmouth daughter. My mother used to say that one day my mouth would get me in big trouble, and it has.

You have to understand that NAN was an organization that followed a very traditional model. The leaders within and around NAN were not just any old neighborhood Joes holding signs. They were historians, and many were members of Dr. King's school of activism. They were raised in the Civil Rights Movement. The organization was filled with pivotal figures. I learned from legends how to activate and make a social impact. If you were in Harlem in the late 1990s and early 2000s, you would meet some of the world's most influential Black thought leaders.

Dr. John Henrik Clarke
Dr. Yosef Ben-Jochannan
Charshee McIntyre
Camille Yarbrough

A lot of times newer leaders are not rooted in the history, and it doesn't diminish their value, but my teachers were historians.

There is a difference when you have an actual connection to the minds of the historians who got us to where we are.

I'm not just speaking about the study of enslavement up until this point. I am talking about the history of Black people around the world, from the origin in Africa and every stop along the way to the Americas. I learned that I had an obligation to address the concerns of the Black diaspora. While we like to create subcategories, separating African Americans from Jamaicans, from Haitians, and so on, we are linked through the diaspora. The only difference between us is the stops the ships made along the way and where our ancestors were forced to get off the boat. There is an African heritage that streamlines us. There is a shared history among Black global citizens, and I learned the significance of that during my time at National Action Network.

THE SACRIFICE OF THE ACTIVIST

The walk of activism is taxing, physically, mentally, and emotionally. The things I witness in the chaos of this fight haunt me. I live in a state of outrage. Physical sometimes, emotional always. The bodies of victims, the injustices, the mamas and sisters in desperate need of support who I try to lift up with words or a hug that can never replenish their souls. Standing toe to toe with armed police officers who would gladly lay me down to stop my message. I absorb all that pain. It seeps into me, and when I'm on, I'm giving it all I have. I'm crying, I'm raging, I'm screaming, I'm doing interviews, I'm marching, I'm taking pepper spray to the face, relocating to the cities where justice is not being served, being arrested, taking death threats, all that. I'm activating on behalf of Black and brown people who are targets of this racist system. When my switch is flipped on, the institution gets all this smoke. Every little bit of courage I have, I leave on the concrete. I will light the streets up in the name of justice, to the point where I miss meals, I lose weight, I've had COVID-19, I miss time with my mother, who recently fell ill, and my father, who is my silent motivator. I miss important moments with my child and every other sacrifice along the way. Most recently I learned to flip the switch off. This fight will kill me if I don't. So, when you see me listening to Cardi B or dancing to Beyoncé's new anthem, or hear me kicking it with my community of followers on social media, give me that. Give me that space to be Tamika, the girl from Harlem, because it's my way of turning off the pain, of letting a little out.

I have learned that I can be an activist and be a regular person too. I deserve to tap into normalcy when I need to. It is what keeps my emotions in check and keeps me sane. I honestly don't know why anyone would choose this life. It is hell some days. They say the definition of insanity is doing the same thing over and over but expecting a different result.

Activism = Insanity

I've marched hundreds of times. I've protested thousands of issues. The short-term result is rarely favorable to my mission, yet I do not quit. This lifestyle is heavy, and the steps are burdensome. I experience letdown after letdown on my pathway toward freedom. I'm targeted. I live in constant concern for my life and the life of my son. There are many adversaries, but the system is too flawed to back down.

I know everyone reading my words can interpret them many ways. Not everyone with this book in their hands looks like me. Let me be clear about who this movement stands for and what we are fighting against. I never stand against humanity. I am for all people who have been disenfranchised, discriminated against, and disrespected. It does not matter what you look like or where you come from. Injustice is injustice, and I lend my voice to that fight. You could be Black, white, Hispanic, Asian, Middle Eastern, man, woman, or members of the LGBTQIA+ community. I want to be your ally. I *am* your ally. And I acknowledge a need to be a better advocate. I try my best to stand for righteousness. The people who march with me, side by side, march against institutions. No person is the enemy. The system is the opposition. The deeply rooted and archaic model that inequitably distributes land, jobs, health care, safety, education, and resources is the issue. America was created around a system that uses suppression to keep power funneled into the hands of a white democracy.

We live in a world where police officers are protected and defended when they murder unarmed Black citizens. We are finally reaching a place where humanity demands that the system be changed. With the frequency and deliberate nature of recent events involving police brutality, empathy for the Black experience has finally begun to arrive. What has been put on display for the world to see is hard to sweep under the rug. Racism and attacks against people of color are woven into the seams of this country. The system is unequivocally flawed and seeded with the intent to disenfranchise and disrupt the growth of Black and brown Americans.

Four
The Rules

THE BURDEN OF BLACKNESS

The performance of being Black in America is exhausting. Putting on the mask of assimilation every day, most likely for eight hours a day if you work within the economic institution, and lowering your Blackness until you return to the perceived safety of the four walls you call home. It's something you've done for so long that you don't even need to practice. You just dial it down a little as soon as you step out your door, because if you don't, your life is at stake. I don't subscribe to that method of survival. I've been in this freedom fight for two decades, and I realize that my undiluted Blackness is worth fighting for. I've committed to the possibility that it's worth dying for. I am who I am, but I understand those who are just surviving while Black the best way they see fit, juggling between their authentic selves and a version of Black that is digestible in a white society. I understand that adaptation, that skill which is developed in order to survive. Being a

41

Black woman is even harder. Malcolm X once called the Black woman the most disrespected person in America.

I can confidently say that the burden of American Blackness is almost unbearable. But don't mistake my meaning. I wouldn't want to be anything else. Black comes with a rhythm that turns our bodies to art when we hear a dope beat. It turns scraps of food that others find useless into feasts large enough to feed entire communities. It transforms poetry plus percussion into an art form all its own: hip-hop. It infuses the way the world thinks of what's cool, of what's cultured, of what's dope. Black people add seasoning to everything we touch, whether it's clothing, music, dance, or art. Our culture is beautiful. I love everything about being a Black woman, from the tint of my skin to the kink of my hair, but despite all these beautiful things, there is a hardship attached to being Black. There are the rules we all must remember to follow in order to get by. Black women know them all too well:

Rule #1: Do not raise your voice when faced with any challenge.
Consequence: They will call you angry.

Rule #2: Do not wear any hairstyle that could be deemed "ethnic" in a professional or scholastic setting. Said styles include braids, locs, Afros, bald heads, natural curl patterns.

Consequence: They will touch your hair, assume you're unkempt, and call you ghetto. In extreme cases, you may be expelled or fired from the institution.

Rule #3: Never admit to or complain about feelings of sadness or claim to be overwhelmed. Always power through extreme levels of pain in silence.
Consequence: They will call you mentally unstable or erratic.

Rule #4: Never ask for help.
Consequence: They will call you lazy or incompetent.

Rule #5: Don't talk back.
Consequence: You will be deemed dangerous.

Rule #6: Don't protest unjust abuse.
Consequence: They will say you hate America.

Rule #7: Always keep your hands in plain sight, either on the dashboard or the steering wheel, and look straight ahead when you get pulled over by the police.
That one is for Black men too, a universal rule.
Consequence: THEY WILL KILL YOU.

THE STREETS OF KENOSHA, WISCONSIN

As I write this, it's August 2020, and the country is mourning yet more state-operated violence. Jacob Blake was shot and paralyzed in Kenosha, Wisconsin, just two days ago. Here I sit, putting pen to paper with the intent of inspiring with my prescription for change, but I can honestly say my voice has grown weary. Despite this book, despite my efforts in the streets of Louisville and Minneapolis, despite demonstrations filling the streets of DC, New York, Chicago, LA, and everywhere else, innocent Black men keep dying at the hands of police. I'm honestly devastated, but we live in a world where vulnerability gets labeled as weakness. Or worse, anger. I don't want to be known as the invincible Black woman. This fight hurts.

Black women in America—Black people, period—live beneath a superstructure of unspoken rules required in order to survive the country where we have always been under attack. We are never to complain or appear weak, no matter the circumstance, because somewhere along the way, doggedness under abuse got rebranded as "Black girl magic." Like we're mythical creatures impervious to pain. No matter how bad something feels, the expectation is of endurance only, never empathy.

I receive death threats almost daily from white-supremacist groups who see me as a loud Black woman they need to shut up. I'm expected to remain strong and silent while I navigate a state of constant terror, uncertainty, anger, and sadness. It's why I trust my vulnerability only with my family, and when I say "family," I extend that to the network of freedom fighters I've built with Until Freedom. They accept my vulnerabilities because they see the day-to-day demands of pulling up to the latest in a series of tragedies every day. In those moments I *wish* I were made of magic. I wish there were some special power I could use to equalize injustice, but it is those moments that expose exactly how human I am. Those moments on the ground are crushing.

At times I feel like no one understands the experience of the Black woman, but then I look at the Black man. While we share the same melanin, our versions of being Black in America present differently. We saw that with seventeen-year-old Trayvon Martin. He was guilty of nothing but being threatening in the eyes of one racist man. If Trayvon were white, he would have made it home that night. There are countless instances of Black men and women whose lives have been snuffed out like they're nothing—most not even recognized beyond a damn local headline. Only in America does a George Zimmerman, the admitted killer of a Black boy, get to sue the victim's family for $100 million.

LOUISVILLE, KENTUCKY, USA

They say history repeats itself. When Jacob Blake was shot, I had already relocated my entire life to Louisville, Kentucky, protesting for months in the streets, for justice in honor of

Breonna Taylor. Her murder is an injustice that is unforgivable. Breonna was one of those brave souls doing her job in the face of a then-emerging global pandemic. March 13, 2020. She was a health care worker, an emergency room technician, serving others. Her payback? Being murdered by police officers who came to her home in the middle of the night to serve a no-knock warrant. Imagine Breonna's last day. Exhausted as the world took its first steps toward figuring out the devastation of COVID-19, making it to the safety of the four walls of her home, and seeing intruders break down her door, disturb her peace, and ultimately take her life. Badge or not, that's murder.

I'd never call the murder of Breonna a "mistake"—the conditions that led to her death were anything but accidental. But what stood out to me was the zealous anger with which the Louisville police department fell in line to defend their colleagues' mishandling of the raid on Breonna Taylor's home. It wasn't enough to say the officers messed up or got caught in the heat of the moment. No, just as we've seen so many times before and since, justification began with disassembling the victim's character. Unable to find anything damaging in her history, the media and law enforcement combed through her personal relationships and those of her acquaintances. The idea was to hold her character accountable to the people around her. When living in an impoverished Black community, everyone is affiliated with someone who has been affected by systemic racism. The War on Drugs produced drug dealers and drug users. Everyone knows that, and most of us who have experienced poverty within the Black community know someone who knows someone who ain't living right. Prosecutors and defenders of police brutality love to use these tenuous ties of affiliation against Black and brown victims like Breonna Taylor. There are political figures and presidents who have been implicated in illegal scandals, photographed with the vilest members of our society, human traffickers and child abusers, but they are not guilty by association. The rule is conveniently applied only when it tarnishes Black people. It always seems anything goes when it comes time to stand behind trigger-happy cops. I know not all cops are racist, not all cops are bad, but the blue wall of silence that ensures few cops ever face any kind of accountability for their actions taints the rest of the pool along with the bad apples. I hear people use that analogy a lot: "A few bad apples don't spoil the bunch." But I disagree wholeheartedly. "A few bad cops" is intolerable. They must all operate from a higher moral code. One bigoted cop is too many. People we trust to carry guns through our neighborhoods, to lay down justice and to make decisions about forcibly denying our citizens' freedom, need to be held to a different standard.

ORIGINAL SACRIFICE

This is where history comes in. It's easy to call out racists and their protectors within the criminal justice system. Less easy is figuring out what can be done about it. Catchphrases and hashtags can raise awareness, but cutting out the sickness of systemic racism needs to start from a place of historical context. These structures weren't built overnight, and they won't go away overnight either. To understand what right-thinking people are up against, we need to understand how we got here.

Murderers have gotten away with extinguishing Black lives for centuries. That's the history America is only now beginning to process and reconcile with. Even our history books have been sanitized to minimize the violence at the center of our country's biography. We must figure out how the foundation of racism was built, because it didn't start with Trayvon Martin or Breonna Taylor.

Black human life is equal to the lives of others. That's what the Constitution guarantees, but the remnants of the time in which our founding documents were written—1787 was a *long* time ago—still color our lives today. Why does it feel like Black lives are *less than,* and always have been *less than,* in America? Because they were. It's written in this country's DNA. Article 1, Section 2, Clause 3:

> Representatives and direct Taxes shall be apportioned among the several States which may be included within this Union, according to their respective Numbers, which shall be determined by adding to the whole Number of free Persons, including those bound to Service for a Term of Years, and excluding Indians not taxed, three fifths of all other Persons.

Three-fifths of all other persons. Less than. Black people have been fractionated by law, dismissed by law, and had our well-being dismissed, by law, from day one. Funnily enough, treating Black people as whole people in this case would have set us back even further. The South wanted to have its cake and eat it too: to keep its slaves, deny them rights, but use their bodies for the purpose of securing representation in Congress. Sometimes you hear enslavement described as America's original sin—"three-fifths" was America's original sacrifice. Two hundred and fifty years later, and we're still trying to get those other two back.

So, let's break it down, because although the Thirteenth Amendment abolished slavery and eradicated this three-fifths compromise, the marginalization never stopped. The spirit of this practice, of only counting some, lives on today. I can't help but think about the running tally of Black people who have been murdered by either racist vigilantes or cops. People like:

MYA HALL—In April 2015, a twenty-seven-year-old transgender Black woman was killed at a National Security Agency guard post after making a wrong turn. Some speculate that she was joyriding with her friend Brittany Fleming after engaging in sex work. The wrong turn led her to take a restricted exit. Her vehicle was shot at, and Mya was killed in the incident. As a Black transgender woman with a checkered history, her death was barely recognized in mainstream media, and when it was mentioned, she was written off because the history of her criminal record was spotlighted over the events that occurred that night. The exit she mistakenly took is a common wrong turn on that road, but for Mya Hall, it was a driving error that cost her life. Hardly anyone ever says her name. It is the plight of too many transgender women, especially trans women of color. Their abuse and murders often go unacknowledged.

NATASHA McKENNA—In 2015, thirty-seven-year-old McKenna, who suffered from bipolar disorder and schizophrenia, was killed by excessive use of a Taser while shackled at the hands and feet. The Virginia medical examiner's official report claimed "excited delirium" contributed to her death, but it was labeled a homicide. Her last words were "You promised you wouldn't kill me." She was killed while in police custody. Her death was ruled to be accidental, and no officers were charged.

PHILANDO CASTILE—In 2016, a thirty-two-year-old man was shot during a traffic stop in St. Anthony Village, Minnesota. Philando Castile held a permit for a firearm he carried in his vehicle. He informed the officer that the permit and weapon were present. The officer shot seven bullets into the car, and five hit Castile, with two piercing his heart. His four-year-old daughter and his girlfriend were in the car. The officer was acquitted and received a $48,500 buyout to voluntarily leave the department.

STEPHON CLARK—In 2018, a twenty-two-year-old man was shot in his grandmother's backyard while police were canvassing a Sacramento, California, neighborhood in search of a suspect. Stephon Clark was unarmed. The police shot him more than twenty times for having a cell phone in his hand. No officers were charged in his murder.

MANUEL ELLIS—In 2020, Manuel Ellis was restrained by Tacoma, Washington, officers using excessive force. His cause of death was homicide by hypoxia—basically, they cut off his air supply. His last words: "I can't breathe." The last words of too many Black men and women. The officers were placed on leave.

No one was held criminally liable in any of these cases. Not one life was counted in the eyes of the justice system, and there are hundreds more cases just like them. I can't help but wonder if there is an unspoken agreement maintained where the powers that be still function by that old three-fifths rule. And think about how many murdered slaves' lives have been lost to history. How many great- and great-great-grandparents of people today—people you work with, speak to, call kin—were murdered without a second thought. Three-fifths.

Consciously or not, suburban America has always tucked the turmoil of the Black experience away inside inner-city zip codes, where it can be left unseen and unrepaired. It's swept under the rug, and when the two sides come face-to-face—let's say, as you saw earlier, at a traffic stop—it's disastrous. Skin color does not make us more likely to bring you harm or commit a crime. When police officers respond to calls and they see Black faces, it ignites fear that heightens the likelihood of aggression on the scene. Two examples come to mind. Deon Kay was a young teenage boy in the District of Columbia. He was shot and killed after brandishing a weapon while running from the police. There was no communication, no attempts to deescalate the situation. Within seconds, Deon Kay was on the ground, bleeding out from a single gunshot. Deon Kay hadn't harmed anyone with his weapon. The only person harmed that day was Deon Kay. Police didn't do the work to figure out why he was carrying a weapon. The police have a moral obligation to do more than point and shoot.

Think about Kyle Rittenhouse, the white seventeen-year-old wannabe superhero who killed two people when he traveled to oppose protesters in Kenosha, Wisconsin, after the Jacob Blake shooting. The police were called to the scene as gunfire erupted in the area. They watched Rittenhouse carry a semi-automatic assault rifle in plain sight. Did they pull their guns, shoot, and ask questions later? Of course not. In fact, they stopped to ask Rittenhouse for directions and let him go on his way after he had already KILLED two people. He was given the benefit of the doubt and allowed to walk free because of his race. There was no fear present when the police approached Rittenhouse. His gun didn't make him a thug, or a threat, or a suspect. They allowed him not only to live but to walk away without asking any questions about his weapon. A Black Kyle Rittenhouse would have been deemed a threat on sight, one great enough to put down without question. If But when Rittenhouse beat murder charges for his killings of Joseph Rosenbaum and Anthony Huber I was crushed, but not surprised. If only Deon Kay had been given the same opportunity to state his case.

THE CENTRAL PARK FIVE

Every day for the past four years, the political atmosphere has been clouded with rhetoric to "Make America Great Again." It's the word "again" for me. I struggle to recall a time when America was ever great in the first place. I can't find it in history books, and most of the people I know can't remember the time period either. Certainly not for America's impoverished, the targeted, the scapegoated. The divisive systems that exist today have always been in place. I remember the first time I realized that race mattered, that my skin made me different, that it made others react to me differently. Every Black person has that moment when racism crashes into them and the realization that there is a stigma to being a Black person in this country. I came to that realization during the trial of the Central Park Five. I was nine years old. My parents were visible activists, so I was nearby as those young boys' lives hung in the balance. I remember their mothers attending rallies in support of a fair investigation and trial. I watched their mothers' hearts break as they asked for help, hearing the stories of what was going on right in my own neighborhood.

Kevin Richardson
Raymond Santana
Antron McCray
Yusef Salaam
Korey Wise

The media named them "The Central Park Five," as if they were some kind of Wild West posse. But I just saw them as boys from around the way. I grew up around kids just like them. I had no idea that they would one day become good friends of mine, but I knew then that if they were white, they wouldn't have been treated unjustly. They would have been given the benefit of reasonable doubt. They were guilty as soon as the police got them to the station; the trial was only a show to make us all feel better about watching these Black lives taken out of circulation. At nine years old, I already knew that my skin color, my hair texture—intrinsic features of my humanity I had no part in choosing—had pinned me as an assumed criminal. An object of suspicion and disdain. For life.

It's a conversation that I had with my own son when I became a mother. It hurt my soul to explain hatred to a child who hadn't yet been tainted by the world. I attempted to make something logical out of illogic. Letting a Black boy know that the world will villainize him, no matter his age, no matter his innocence, and preparing him to behave in a way that will keep him alive. It's a conversation every Black parent in America is forced to have with their children. Balancing the responsibility of teaching a child to love who they are, what they look like, and where they come from versus what society thinks of them. The confusion of innocent eyes, the pain behind discovering that there is a thread of hate woven into the very fabric of the land we call home. Yes, this is our home. If we had the ability to reach beyond the history of enslavement, most of us would welcome the opportunity to immerse ourselves in our true ethnicity. But that opportunity was stripped away from us. Where most can tap into their lineage, whether it be Irish, German, Mexican, Chinese, or Indian, Black Americans don't know what precedes enslavement. We aren't ever taught what comes before the shackles, the cotton fields, and the whips. Our true history was tossed overboard and lost somewhere in the middle of the Atlantic Ocean during the Middle Passage, a journey 12.5 million enslaved Africans endured before being sold on an auction block.[1]

I can only scratch the very surface of the journey because if we really talked about more than 246 years of enslavement, this book would never end. What I will do is talk about the decisions—the moments and legislation in the history we do know—that have stunted the progression of Black America. Moments when racist ideologies, corrupt politics, and biased systems created what we now brush off as "lazy," "entitled," "undeserving."

WHERE
WE ARE

Five

The U.S. vs. Black America

A TRAP BY DESIGN

Laws are meant to protect people. Society agrees upon some standards to establish order and give communities ways in which to govern themselves and their property. And laws require punishment. A rule with no consequence doesn't hold much weight. It's a simple enough setup, but from the very beginning of the establishment of this country, our laws have been applied with prejudice. Laws created and imposed with the intention to protect can be used just as easily to contain and undermine. When laws are written with the intention to target and disrupt a community of people, instead of with the intention to prevent harm, they become more bricks laid into the foundation of institutional racism. And in modern America, the favored method of applying disruptive law has always been the War on Drugs.

The agenda and racist beliefs of our founding fathers set the tone for generations of mistrust between the Black community and political leaders. The sentiment of a hierarchy in which Black citizens occupy the lowest slot on the political totem pole has been inherited since the very first president held office. This never really went away, but you could argue it had gone into a period of relative hibernation in the 1960s. John F. Kennedy and Lyndon B. Johnson had overseen a broad expansion of the civil and economic rights of people of color in this country. Far from perfect, they had at the very least not stood in the way of progress pushed by an era of leaders like Dr. Martin Luther King, Jr. and Whitney Young. But a different kind of book will teach you that every action produces a reaction in response. America's reaction was President Richard Nixon. Beyond the racial reckoning of the 1960s, Nixon also took office during one of our most volatile wars, Vietnam. America was losing troops by the tens of thousands, and the Black community had taken a vocal position against its continuance.

Black Americans felt like they were being drafted and forced to fight in a "white man's war." To fight for a country that denied Blacks basic human rights was beyond immoral, yet Black men were drafted by the thousands. Black men made up 11 percent of the nation's population in 1965, at the start of the war, but were 25 percent of the casualties of that war.[1] Black soldiers were disproportionately assigned to dangerous combat units, resulting in major loss of life.[2]

THE WAR ON DRUGS

Sammy Younge, Jr., was among the Black troops who served in Vietnam, yet he was murdered by a white man in Macon

County, Alabama, for using a whites-only restroom in 1966.[3] Now, keep in mind the Civil Rights Act of 1964 outlawed public segregation, so Samuel Younge, Jr., broke no laws. Still, a Black member of the navy was murdered for using the wrong restroom in the Jim Crow South. His killer, Marvin Segrest, was acquitted by an all-white jury. This is not that long ago. I guarantee you know someone at your workplace or in your family who wasn't just alive in 1966 but was a very conscious adult functioning in that same society. Black leaders, including the late, great John Lewis, protested not only Younge's death but the conflict of having Black soldiers in Vietnam. Black men were fighting a war of their own on domestic soil. The political protests were anti-war, and President Nixon sought to disrupt the strength growing in the Black community. The launch of Nixon's reign over the War on Drugs was one of the most disruptive political tactics contrived against Black America in history. It certainly sounds like a noble stance to take as a country's leader: Nobody wants a country plagued by drugs, right? Taking a firm stance to keep the streets of the United States clean of narcotics is a very presidential thing to do. It's a policy that administrations are remembered for, right? Nixon's agenda, however, was laser-targeted to cripple the Black community.

His administration created a narrative that heroin use was running rampant in the Black community, and he used that narrative to incarcerate Black men by the thousands. The number of nonviolent drug convictions skyrocketed. In a 1994 interview, Nixon's domestic policy chief, John Ehrlichman, confirmed the racial motivation behind their War on Drugs legislation:

We couldn't make it illegal to either be against the war or Black, but by getting the public to associate marijuana with hippies and Blacks with heroin, and then criminalizing both heavily, we could disrupt those communities. We could arrest their leaders, raid their homes, break up their meetings, and vilify them night after night on the evening news. Did we know we were lying about the drugs? Of course we did.[4]

Then the 1980s hit, and the crack cocaine epidemic spawned under a different leader, President Ronald Reagan. Although the CIA still denies it, it's often speculated[5] that cocaine was planted in South Central LA, where the CIA used local gangs to distribute and sell it for profit. The profits were then used to fund contra-rebel forces in Nicaragua determined to overthrow the Nicaraguan government.[6]

The price of cocaine, however, was unaffordable. But local gangs soon figured out how to stretch their supplies of the higher-quality powder by transforming it into a cheaper, more addictive rock form, crack cocaine.

Crack, in the context of poverty, devastated the Black community. The crisis saw loving mothers, now addicts, pushed into selling their bodies for the drug. It led young men with aptitudes for a career in business to test their gifts in the wildly lucrative drug game. When there were no jobs available, no systems in place to create wealth within inner-city neighborhoods like Harlem, where I grew up, young men used crack as their enterprise. Crack cocaine tore through the Black family unit like a hurricane. The War on Drugs became even more crippling when Reagan passed the Anti–Drug Abuse Act of 1986. The law enforced mandatory minimum sentences for drug possession, with stricter sentencing attached to those in possession of crack cocaine. Meanwhile, powdered cocaine—a so-called white man's drug popular with celebrities, in finance circles, and in the downtown party scene—evaded the harshest punishments. The more affordable and widely available crack cocaine inundated the inner cities, where Black and brown people took the biggest blow from these new laws. The sentences for being caught with it were a hundred times harsher than those for cocaine. The disparity was a hundred to one. Possession of five grams of crack is punishable by five years in prison. It takes five hundred grams of powdered cocaine to get the same sentence. Same drug, different faces. That is bias written into law.

Families were torn apart as prisons filled with Black men, leaving behind single Black women to raise babies alone. Once crack took hold of Black neighborhoods, it didn't let go. Addiction plagued the 1980s and 1990s, contributing to the mass breakdown of the Black family unit. Homicide rates doubled during the crack epidemic. Mothers strung out on the drug gave birth to a generation of children forced to deal with crack cocaine's effects. Some were born addicted, and those who were not still faced the residual effects of a community riddled with the drug's impact. The rate of Black children who went into foster care nearly doubled.[7] These were organized plots put in place by two of our nation's leaders to debilitate an entire segment of the population. It was an institutional trap that only further proved the racist foundations that lace our political and judicial system. Black America has yet to fully recover. And to be clear, none of the people responsible were ever held accountable.

CHECK THIS! (OWNED OR DEAD)

Combing through a few hundred years of oppression feels brutal, I know, but we can't avoid it anymore if we want to repair the wounds. Acts of legislation are complex notions that are meant to affect the masses. You probably skimmed that Nixon administration talk. I might have done that myself if I were you. But those are the underlying facts for you to use when you need them. Now let me give it to you in a way you can relate to. At the micro level. Person to person. Human to human. Heart to heart.

Numbers paint a sterile picture of how drugs, single parenthood, and violence impact the Black community. Numbers can be too detached. They give you a top-down picture instead of personalizing the effect these laws have on real people. Society has a way of measuring effectiveness with numbers, but they're cold, merely black ink on paper. They remove the consequence from the action. If you're looking at the numbers, analyzing violent crime rates inside Black neighborhoods, discussing legislation, speaking about drug addiction within the community, you want to see numbers that make sense. You want to see ink that makes you feel safe. That makes you feel like the system is working when you see that arrests of Black offenders are high and crime in your suburban bubble is low. They help you justify life sentences for young boys because they come from a place where violent crime rates are sky-high. The numbers make you look at mandatory minimum sentencing and think that it works, that they're just.

The numbers are wrong. Analytics can't measure humanity. Black people cannot be represented by numbers. There are too many extraordinary circumstances contributing to the numbers that reflect our neighborhoods. Black men are disproportionately affected by systemic racism, yet we rarely hear their side of the story. America doesn't see Black men unless they're owned or dead. Ownership comes in many forms. Whether Black men are athletes who perform under billion-dollar franchises owned by white men, or whether they are inmates working for pennies an hour doing the work that governments refuse to pay citizens to do, it's all a form of belonging to the institution. Those are the only Black men acknowledged by society. The super Black man who makes the institution wealthier by tossing a ball, or the Black man seen as a "thug" and put in jail or in a grave. They don't see Black men as scholars, as engineers, as doctors. They see Black men as numbers, and although the numbers may be technically accurate, they don't tell a full story.

While I have the microphone, I am obligated to do my part to humanize Black men, to give life to their pain, because America seems to think we are all complacent in the dysfunction that plagues our community. America tends to think we don't aspire to rise from the concrete jungles we've been placed and trapped in.

Next I want to tap into the hearts of Black men, some who have never shared their experience, their trauma, the reasoning behind their choices. It isn't just white America; Black women also sometimes struggle to hear and empathize with Black men. Other communities misunderstand that unprocessed trauma sits behind their stature, their Blackness, the stern brows, the defensive demeanors. The exterior is a defense mechanism to protect them from a world that is designed to inflict harm.

The numbers miss that part. They're unfairly stacked. It's about the experiences, those nuances I spoke about earlier. That's what this part is about. Some things must be humanized to understand how we got here, to dissect how the mere presence of a Black man became something that other races feared. The problem is, I don't think I can tell that part. I don't have full access to their story, their strife. They must tell their own. Let me introduce you to my brother, an important partner in my work. I have to let him tell their truth in his way.

Mysonne "The General" Linen. You've seen him standing beside me during 2020's racial reckoning. He is a brother to me. He works alongside us in the fight for justice at Until Freedom. He is a rapper. A freedom fighter. A father. And guess what? He's a convicted felon. That's right. You heard me correctly. Black life isn't one-dimensional, and Black activists come from all walks of life. There is no prerequisite to enroll in this modern movement.

Mysonne is a Black man who fell into the systemic traps set by legislation like the 1994 Crime Bill. He was found guilty of a crime he didn't commit. He was present but uninvolved in the assault and robbery of a cabdriver. Mysonne had no priors, no arrest record, was enrolled in college, and had just signed his first record deal when the sentence came down. He was a perfect candidate for the system to give a second chance, but not enough young Black men receive those. He was punished for the crime and served seven years in prison. He is a person I trust with my life, a father to three Black boys, and my co-founder in Until Freedom. He looks like a statistic, like another Black boy who the system swallowed whole. He is so much more, and the circumstances he was born into do not define the character of the man he is today.

BY MYSONNE LINEN

I'm a Black man. I say that with the utmost pride, even though I know we are the most hated and misunderstood being that exists. It's crazy to me, the way the world doubts Black men. I've never been in a situation in my entire life where I felt like I could depend on someone. Consistency has been evasive in my life since I was a young child. From teachers, to women I've dated, to my mother. I've never been able to completely trust that the person who loves me and is in front of me today will be there tomorrow. No matter who I encountered, no matter how much I needed them, no matter how much I believed in them, there was always the sting of unmet expectations. Revoked promises. Shallow commitments. The depth of a young boy's heart is dependent on the source filling it. I could always touch bottom because the people I expected to pour into me disappeared. I learned to depend on me, to stand on the promises I made myself, after life introduced me to the tender feeling of disappointment as a kid.

I was born and raised in the Highbridge section of the Bronx. Now, my mother is a woman of resilience, strength, and integrity. She is unlike anyone I have ever known, but she worked hard to battle systemic traps, specifically drugs and poverty, to become the woman she is today. You see, my mother was sixteen years old when she had me. She was a child herself, suddenly with the responsibility of taking care of a baby. I guess that's where the cycle began. I was born in the late 1970s, so the crack era painted the landscape of my adolescence, and it was rough. Drugs were everywhere. I would see people I looked up to, people who went to work every day, who welcomed me into their homes to play with their kids one day . . . and the next day they would be different. Drugs turned them into something that I didn't recognize. Different versions of themselves. They looked less alive, if I'm honest. They were walking, talking beings, but somehow they looked lifeless, like the drugs had taken ahold of them and were not going to let go until there was nothing left. My dad looked like that most days. My mom too, and although I couldn't identify their addiction at first sight as a child, it was crystal clear in hindsight. They would fight. Every day I witnessed domestic violence. The yelling, the physical abuse my mom endured, it was constant. My father would beat my mother and turn into a stranger I hardly recognized. I didn't know at the time he was high. I just knew he was mean, but the chaos was so consistent that it became a part of my routine.

Sports were an escape, and I was a smart kid, but my teachers misunderstood me. I had a lot going on at home, but nobody invested the time to take a closer look. They just saw an angry little Black boy. I'll never forget my third-grade teacher telling me I would be dead before I was eighteen years old. I can't imagine any white young boy being spoken to like that. I was eight and already written off because of behavioral problems. A man who was supposed to inspire me to use education as a key to unlock the door out of poverty had sentenced me to die. It got so bad that they sent me to a psychiatrist, starting a formal file identifying me as a kid who needed to be fixed, a kid who had something "wrong" with him. I was just a child balancing extreme trauma with school. My problems at home didn't leave room for focus in school. I was smart, but I was terrified. While my classmates were learning multiplication, I was worried about what I would encounter when I made it home.

At Until Freedom, we fight against systems that oppress Black people, legislation that targets Black communities with the intent to disrupt and destroy the Black family. The War on Drugs and the placement of cocaine in our neighborhoods tore my family apart. I wonder often what life would have been like had my parents never encountered drugs. Addiction crippled my family. I lost my father to a heroin overdose when I was eleven years old. We found him on our couch three days after he had already passed. I will never forget how his eyes were stuck wide open and his body was deformed by rigor mortis. It was one of the most chilling moments of my life. I became the man of the house. I was my mother's oldest child but still just a boy—and yet the burden of caring for an entire household had been passed down to me. It wasn't my responsibility, but I had to do it. If I didn't, my little sister's life would fall apart. Life was already hard, but after my father's overdose, it got worse.

Throughout my entire teenage years, my mother was addicted to drugs. My sister and I had to fend for ourselves. There was no food, because the welfare card my mother received went straight to the drug dealers to pay for her habit when she didn't have cash. I got into a lot of fights with them. I was a teenage kid fighting men in their twenties and thirties, because when they came to collect the debt my mom owed, it took food from my and my sister's mouths. It was either fight them or starve. I found myself in those situations often. The heartbreak of knowing my mom was high and the frustration of just wanting her to stop. I would stand up to the dealers and tell them to stop selling to my mother. They felt my pain. They could hear my passion. I was willing to go to war against them just to keep my mother off drugs. It didn't work. No matter how many fights I got into, there was always a new dealer willing to take the money. Her addiction lasted for years. Through this period, she birthed two more sons, so I became the eldest of four. I had to take care of us all. What was I going to do? How was I going to make sure not only I survived, but my siblings survived as well? The only way I saw others making it in the projects was by selling drugs. What other choice did I have? Go to school? I was smart, and I could have excelled in an educational environment, but that was a plan for the long term. That would have paid off eventually. I needed help now. My sister and brothers had to eat now. I could either spend eight hours a day in a school where teachers misunderstood me, or spend eight hours doing something that would put food on the table for my sister and brothers today. That's a no-brainer.

School didn't feel like a place I belonged. The education system in the Black community is a joke. Black boys are labeled, and the process of institutionalization starts as soon as they mistake our trauma for misbehavior. A third-grade little boy doesn't have aggression issues, he is hurt. How do I know? Because I was that boy. I was sitting in a classroom with the burden of the world on my shoulders. I needed help. I needed support. Instead, I received judgment and misdiagnoses for things that were beyond my control. School was not an escape for me. It felt like a cage. I had all this pent-up emotion, all these questions about the world and my place in it, all these burdens that I would have loved to be distracted from by learning about something new, but I was not stimulated. Why? Not because I didn't want to learn, but because I didn't learn in the linear way that the system presents information. American school systems are not designed to benefit Black students. They barely even recognize Black culture. I didn't fit in an educational environment that expected me to sit in one place for hours. How? When I was used to running, used to fighting, used to moving fast, thinking fast, to survive. They wanted me to slow down, to sit at one desk, in one room, for hours, listening to people talk past me. Black children, especially Black boys, do not thrive in that environment. We learn through movement, through dance, through song. We are interactive learners. The way we are taught does not stimulate our attributes or awaken our psyches. We're expected to be robotic, to be slaves to an educational model that puts us into the workforce as employees, not CEOs, punching clocks at nine-to-five jobs, making someone else—more often than not, a white someone else—rich while we work menial positions just to stay afloat. So I stopped going. I turned to the streets even when I knew I was too smart to be there, even though I knew what it felt like to be the child of two addicts, I still did it because I needed to. I grew up watching everyone in my neighborhood struggle except for the men who sold drugs. There was no other model for success.

I didn't make the choice because I wanted to; I needed an immediate savior from poverty, from starvation. My little brothers and my sister needed clothes, they needed shoes, they needed someone to depend on. I knew how important it was to have somebody who would be there, who would make things right. As the oldest, I didn't have that due to my mother's addiction, so I did what I had to do to make sure they were taken care of. I couldn't let them come to me for something and not have it. I wouldn't be one more person disappointing them. I didn't step into criminality to hurt anyone. Nobody is born aspiring to do crime. It was a secondhand skill I picked up by seeing it every day, being around it, having it in my home, on every corner, watching it happen before my eyes. And crime is a product of societal definitions that tell us what is wrong and what is an appropriate response—such as prison—for things we do. But living in the hood, we know that many things considered a crime aren't harmful to anyone, they're about our survival. But our survival has become criminalized, and our community is often punished for surviving. I can see why, to someone who knows nothing about poverty, it is considered vile, but if you've never felt your stomach touch your back or worn shoes after they were two sizes too small because that was all you had, you can't relate to my struggle. Both the usage and selling of drugs were programmed in my daily existence from the day I was born, so to you that's a crime, to me it was a job, a risky one, but one that made living in hell a little more bearable. It was normal, and I was tired of going without things I needed to have even a modest life. I wasn't chasing riches, because I never planned to be involved in drugs long enough to get rich. I just didn't want to suffer anymore. I was raised in a jungle, and in that environment, you have to survive. You do things to ensure that you live another day. I never wanted to be king of that jungle, I just did not want to die there. I wanted security and safety for my family.

I risked my life to save theirs because I was used to being unprotected. Black men are endangered regardless. If I were a straitlaced Harvard graduate, a cop could still look at me and see a life worth taking. I would still be a symbol of fear. My skin, a label that incriminates me before I even commit a crime. America doubts Black men. You have to work immeasurably hard to fight against those doubts. Black men have to prove everything before being given anything. We have to prove that we deserve to be in regular classrooms instead of diagnosed with ADHD and other learning disabilities and lumped into special education courses. We have to prove that we're innocent even if we've never been involved in criminalized activity before. Sometimes it doesn't even matter if we're guilty, we're locked up just because we fit the description, not of a suspect but of what danger looks like in the heads of a fearful cop. We have to prove that we are unarmed and without malice, and we have to prove it swiftly, before a cop decides to shoot first and ask questions later.

But we better not move too quickly in reaching for that wallet when they ask who we are, because that can also end fatally for us. When people see Black men, they assume the worst, and we have to work against that assumption in everything we do. The way we walk, the way we talk, the clothes we choose. It's all under a lens used to justify society's suspicions. Guilty until proven guilty. That is the Black male experience. We're brought up in an environment that promotes death. Every turn of every corner has death lurking, waiting, to claim another Black life. So we adapt, and we learn to navigate within that dangerous space. We learn to be tough so that we aren't targets for violence, and yes, it's terrifying, but you can't ask for help. You can't go to the teachers at school because they already think you're a problem, and if they do offer to help, they're going to take you from your mama because she's living wrong. You can't expect your mother to help because she's living with her own demons, she was a child when she had a child, so you learn to depend on yourself. You can't go to your daddy because he isn't around, in my case he was dead, but here's something you may not know: In many cases, fathers *can't* live in the same house as their children because welfare won't allow a complete family unit to receive assistance. Of course, Mama needs the benefits more than she needs Daddy, so he's out and probably too ashamed to come around because he can't even provide for his family. So Black men learn to depend on no one. I learned to depend on myself. I built myself up to protect myself, to feed myself, to do everything and anything possible to stay alive.

By the time I realized I was being everything that society labeled me, I was on my way to jail. The options America presents to Black men are traps that lead to our extinction or our enslavement. The design of this country and the pockets of decayed land they give Black people to exist in don't make room for life. There is no living happening in the projects. When you're inside a burning building and you're facing pain and inevitable death, you take the nearest exit. You don't care if the window you take to get out is four stories above the ground, you'll jump out of it, just to escape. That's how we end up in the streets. That's how we end up hurting our communities. To survive, you harden yourself, because vulnerability equals death. So I feign strength, even when I'm terrified, even when I'm weak. Black men have to be strong at all times. There are no days off. There is no moment of respite. I'm Black all the time. I'm public enemy number one all the time. I'm exhausted. Every time another Black man is gunned down by police brutality, I build that hardened wall higher, because if it comes crumbling down and I allow myself to feel the weight of what it means to be a Black man, the burden will crush me. The Black man's greatest burden is to see light within himself when the rest of the world has committed him to darkness. America has to acknowledge that light. It has to contribute to sparking that light; investing in the Black community to ensure that the environment promotes life instead of death. You cannot expect someone who is starving to be peaceful. You cannot expect someone raised up in trauma not to engage in escapism by way of narcotics. You cannot create communities where there are food deserts and expect them to be nonviolent. You have to change the circumstances that young Black men grow up in. Remove the stimuli of desperation to cultivate a different result. Give us the same proximity to success that you give everyone else. Give Black men a chance before condemning us to death.

Victor Hugo, the famous poet, once said, "If the soul is left in darkness, sins will be committed. The guilty one is not he who commits the sin, but the one who causes the darkness."

––––––––––––

Men like Mysonne come up with impossible odds against them. The burden of Mysonne's upbringing is identical to that of millions of boys across America, but their stories go untold.

The only way their faces reach you is when they encounter bad fortune. There is no outrunning your environment in this situation. You either adapt or you die, but adaptation creates a stereotype that society uses to lock Black men up and throw away the key. If mandatory minimum sentencing was the trapdoor for Black men in our society, the 1994 Crime Bill was the lock and key.

The Violent Crime Control and Law Enforcement Act[8] was the largest crime control bill in U.S. history. The bill was signed into law by 42nd President Bill Clinton and authored by our 45th, President, Joe Biden. The bill was highly damaging to the Black community. The bill helped to accelerate mass incarceration. It focused on strict punitive action over rehabilitation, and since minimum mandatory sentencing and drugs were already plaguing the Black community, adding this legislation on top of those problems only dug the hole deeper.

Harms of 1994 Crime Bill

- Enacted so-called truth in sentencing, which makes it mandatory for a convicted felon to serve at least 85 percent of his/her sentence; forbids the acceleration of parole for thousands.
- Allowed children thirteen and older who commit violent crimes to be prosecuted as adults.
- Created the three-strike rule for repeat offenders, sentencing them to an automatic life sentence without the possibility of parole.

- Banned prisoners from using Federal Pell Grant money to further their education behind bars.
- Allocated $9.7 billion to the building of more state prisons nationwide.
- Funded the hiring of a hundred thousand more police officers with the intent to place them in inner-city neighborhoods to combat crime.
- Gave states incentives to make their laws more punitive.

The 1994 Crime Bill reinforced racist legislation and laid out an aggressive approach to policing that has kept the Black community in shambles. Imagine if that money and commitment had been invested in the rehabilitation of marginalized communities. If prisons focused on decriminalizing their incarcerated, building up the résumés and skill sets of offenders instead of dehumanizing them. The Crime Bill flooded the streets with more cops. Crime isn't out of control because we don't have enough police officers, it's uncontrollable because the community is not nurtured. If you plant seeds of order, seeds of opportunity, they will grow. The Black community will rise when given the opportunity to flourish. Building more prisons doesn't do anything but create a demand for more inmates to fill them. Black men have been disproportionately imprisoned since way before this bill passed into law, but the bill was an escalation of the prejudice that Black people face within the American justice system. It was the Democratic Party's attempt to prove they could match the Republicans' reputation for being tough on crime, but it solidified the government's use of enforcement as the upgraded model for enslavement in America. A Black child born in America has a one-in-three chance of going to prison.[9] Compare that to one in seventeen for white children.

People who commit what have been identified as crimes aren't the only ones affected by institutional racism and state violence. Women and children are affected as well. Welfare reform is a program designed to help families who live under the poverty line, but it is also a weapon used to weaken and harm Black families—as if locking up our Black men and our civil rights leaders weren't enough. As if infusing inner-city neighborhoods with drugs weren't enough. As if taking away the family structure by locking up the patriarchs of a community weren't enough. America wasn't done with the Black community. Another way to disenfranchise a group of people from the majority is to oust them from resources needed to obtain wealth. The welfare system in this country has a long-standing reputation for discriminating against Black families, specifically women, by pushing the qualifications to receive aid outside of the reach of Black mothers. It's a political tactic that controls who receives aid. While the welfare system is stereotypically seen as a program manipulated and overexerted by Black women, it was designed with racist intent to purposefully exclude the Black family.

Ironically, welfare is often associated with the image of the lazy welfare queen, undoubtedly a Black woman, who takes advantage of taxpayers by relying on government assistance. The term was coined in the 1970s to perpetuate the assumption that Black women abused the system, but history tells us a much different story. From its inception, Black women have been discouraged from receiving benefits from government welfare programs. As you know, I come with receipts. Let's look at the different programs over time that were designed with racist barricades that hindered the survival of Black families.[10]

Early 1900s	Mothers' Pension Program Provided solely to white women and governed locally. The term "suitable homes" prevented Black mothers from receiving aid.
1935	The New Deal Language was removed from social security that barred racial discrimination, leaving local administrators open to bias.
1935 to Post– World War II	Aid to Dependent Children (ADC) Women were disqualified if they received any assistance from a live-in adult male.
1950s	Employable Mother Rule Discouraged out-of-wedlock births in African American women and forced them into menial servitude jobs.
1996 to present	Personal Responsibility and Work Opportunity Reconciliation Act (PRWORA) and Temporary Assistance for Needy Families (TANF) Encouraged work requirements in order to qualify for assistance. Withheld benefits more often from Black applicants due to this.

Access to assistance has been historically denied to Black families, and that has gotten even worse in recent years.[11] The "no man in the house" law fragmented the Black family. A woman was forced to choose between maintaining a complete family unit or feeding her children, and it isn't by chance that the law was enforced heavily in regard to Black women. Often caseworkers would pop up in the middle of the night to make sure no father was in the home. This left Black women to parent alone and to form an independence that has become the ingrained mentality in the Black community: the "I don't need a man" narrative. Black women don't even realize it's a circumstance that was forced upon them, not necessarily one that Black men chose. Black men didn't choose to leave their families. They aren't deadbeats who don't care enough to stick around for their children. They were pushed out by racist laws that were designed to tear the Black family apart and keep them impoverished.

President Barack Obama tried to counter this history by removing the work requirements of the TANF legislation, but one president is not enough to combat an institution built on a foundation of inequality constructed over decades.

Even in my position as a spokesperson for some in Black America, I am still taken aback by the scale of this country's racial inequity. By the creativity with which society has been constructed to maintain the existing racial hierarchy, where white stays on top and everyone else fights for what's left over. As a Black woman, I see the signs of this hierarchy all around me every day. In the ways we're treated. In the ways we are represented and punished within our legal system. In the ways we are (not) accommodated in health care. In the conditions of our children's education. In the ways our applications are viewed on the job. In the ways we are disqualified for loans for businesses and homeownership. I see it on the news when another Black man is gunned down by police. I see it in the neighborhoods of Louisville, Kentucky, where I spent much of 2020 advocating for Breonna Taylor, where Black people live in food deserts. I see it in something as simple as the pavement I walk on in the inner city, where it's unkempt, pockmarked, and left to rot, while affluent suburbia's is manicured and smooth. We are so numb as a society to these disparities that we've normalized egregious maltreatment and neglect. It shouldn't take something as drastic as an 8:46 knee to a neck to wake us up.

History is something we can't change. It's already written. But the future is still pending, and we have the power to effect change. At the beginning of this book, I spoke about the rules to being a Black woman, the not being allowed to express emotion or be angry. Well, I am angry. I'm the definition of an angry Black woman. By the last of these pages, I hope it angers you too. Change requires us to be angry, for us to be loud, for us to disrupt. Together. You must ask yourself: Will you join the freedom fight?

Six

The Roots of Rebellion

ON THE FRONT LINES

As I stand on the front lines, organizing, protesting, and demanding justice, I sometimes grow weary. It's easy to feel discouraged by the obstacles ahead. Picture this, little ol' me, standing front and center, bullhorn in hand, with waves of people from all over the country beside me. We're chanting for freedom. We're taking it to the front lawns of the prosecuting attorneys who refuse to bring charges against cops who take Black lives. We're occupying parks, we're creating petitions, we're taking over city blocks, and then I look out and I see hundreds of police officers in front of me. I see them in full SWAT gear, with artillery designed to fight wars. I see military-style tanks on city streets, waiting and ready to rip through crowds of nonviolent protesters. I see armor and shields and weapons and an unmoved opposition.

Yes, I grow weary on the front lines. I'm sometimes forced to question what the point of our work really is. What hope is there when something as simple as a nonviolent assembly brings out militarized police? The police meet our pain with their aggression. Instead of offering understanding and compassion, the police tax our dollars, wield against us the weapons we paid for, and enter our communities not as liaisons but as an occupying force. They arrive with the intention to punish. It's discouraging. To not be heard when the message is so undeniably clear is hurtful, but resilience is a requirement of the freedom fighter. It always has been. I'm not the first, I am just one of many who have accepted the baton to continue our race toward equality.

The birth of the Black activist is hard to trace. Modern history books would lead you to believe that enslavement in the South was almost civil. Enslaved people were not free, of course, but there was at least an understanding that it was in the owners' best interest to keep their property in good conditions—right? That those slaves who gave birth to their masters' progeny of rape were treated kindly—the "house Negroes," at least, correct? That the reality never exactly reached the heights of inhumanity we might imagine. In one telling, at least they were clothed, sheltered, and fed, right?

Wrong. Black American enslavement was a systemic practice of dehumanization, murder, rape, and torture for the purpose of capitalism and hierarchy.

African Americans come from a tradition of survival. Not simply laboring in the sun, denied the luxuries of leisure, but mostly left to their own devices. No. Survival. Just stepping foot on American soil meant you were a survivor. Untold numbers of enslaved Africans died along the journey to the New World, whether to disease, to famine, to the sea, or to torture dealt out by the slavers themselves. African slaves who survived the perils of the Middle Passage were the strongest of those abducted. Their bodies overcame unimaginably difficult conditions for months during transit. The years of labor and torture to follow ensured that those remaining were even more resilient and strong-willed. That strength fuels the freedom fight of Black Americans today.

It's difficult to trace where Black activism began. Obviously, no one in bondage is agreeable; no slaves wanted to be a part of the system they were trapped in. Even the men and women who refused to leave Africa in bondage and chose sudden death somewhere across the Atlantic can be considered activists. Their suicides were indeed a revolt against the immoral act of enslavement. Even the hum of songs of freedom as slaves picked cotton was a form of resistance. For each lash to every back, for each body that hung from every tree, for each woman raped by every master, for each baby snatched from its mother's embrace, there was an unspoken resistance. The braided hairstyles that I spoke of earlier— you know, the ones that little Black girls are expelled from school for wearing because they violate "dress code"—even the history of those styles was an expression of resistance, often worn by enslaved women to indicate a road map to freedom and hiding seeds to be used as food along the journey. Enslaved mothers who killed their newborn babies to keep them from being generational property of their masters . . . activists.

Even smaller acts of defiance can be considered activism. Breaking field tools, fleeing to neighboring plantations, interrupting work production in any way possible. The reaction to injustice has always been resistance, then and NOW. To the free Black community of the modern day, it is hard to fathom that nearly four million slaves remained in bondage for so long. White masters were outnumbered by the slaves they owned, so it would make sense to revolt together and overpower whites in the South.

It wasn't the physical dominance that kept slaves compliant. It was the mental chains that kept the order of the South before the Civil War began. The mental conditioning of African slaves might be even more of an atrocity than the physical. Wives separated from their husbands. Children ripped from their mother's breast and sold off to other slave masters. Men and women whipped in public as a deterrent to stop runaways. Women raped by their master and then mentally taunted and tortured by their master's wife. Slaves were mutilated, disfigured, and dismembered for being disobedient. All these acts were forms of mental enslavement, mental conditioning. Chains weren't needed, because slaves were mentally captured. To work up the courage to plan or show any form of defiance took years. It wasn't a decision that slaves came to lightly. This act of organizing and protesting that I do today is an extension of their sacrifice, because when they protested, when they revolted, the consequence was death. Freedom or nothing at all was the choice early activists made.

Early Activism = Slave Rebellions

SLAVE REVOLT	YEAR
Cato's Conspiracy	1739
Haitian Revolution	1791
Gabriel's Conspiracy	1800
German Coast Uprising	1811
Denmark Vesey	1822
Nat Turner Rebellion	1831
Harper's Ferry Raid	1859

History is filled with people who gave their lives to their respective movements. Leaders like Dr. Martin Luther King, Jr., and Malcolm X are the ones who haven't been erased from the pages of history books, although we only get around to that section for twenty-eight days every February. I respect their teachings, and I'm grateful for their contributions, but they aren't the ones who shaped this little Harlem girl. Too often activism is seen as a man's sport. Black culture is filled with so many strong, prominent, and charismatic male leaders that often the movements are designed solely around one face . . . a Black male face. Entire movements have been built using a Black man as the nucleus holding it all together, when really there are many elements, many faces, behind the scenes, contributing to the success and viability of the mission of freedom. While I'm so thankful for all these movements, and while I have learned much from watching them shape history,

I reject the sexist notion that says activism is always dependent on a "great man."

It was the women freedom fighters who lit a fire in my soul. It was the Angela Davises, the Sojourner Truths, and the Assata Shakurs of the world. While fighting for both civil rights and, undoubtedly, their respect among men, the women leaders took just as much risk but received little of the recognition. There was no ego involved when women strapped on their boots and lent their lives to the movement. There was no recognition to receive. Just a belief and passion in the quest toward the liberty of Black America.

Ella Josephine Baker is one whose legacy I'm trying to fulfill today. The lesser-known figure, the one who stood behind Dr. Martin Luther King, Jr., but whose impact was just as mighty, is the legacy I look to for inspiration when I feel like my voice is unheard. When I glance at the past and the placement of women in our society in the 1940s, it is of no surprise that Ella Baker ruffled feathers. A woman of action—one with brown skin, at that—could be only as significant as the men around her.[1] While Dr. King was known as the beacon for hope and renowned for his nonviolent approach to activism, it was Ella Baker who convinced the Black community to stand behind him. A leader is only as strong as the people's belief that they can obtain equality. While Dr. King gave grand speeches about hopes and dreams and captured the big moments of the Civil Rights Movement, it was Ella Baker who went door-to-door, convincing people that the dream was achievable. While

Dr. King was the house that encompassed the Black desire to obtain equality, Ella Baker was the foundation sitting beneath it. She joined the NAACP in 1940 and helped an entire generation of young leaders discover their voice, shaping their leadership, teaching them to be democratic in their approach to activism.[2] One of her early students was Rosa Parks. In three short years, Ella Baker became the national director of branches for the organization. She became president of the New York branch of the NAACP in 1952. Ms. Baker was all speed, no brakes, in her pursuit for equal rights. By 1957, she had helped organize the Southern Christian Leadership Conference (SCLC) with the hope of creating an organizing base for Dr. Martin Luther King, Jr. She served as executive director of the SCLC, where she helped mobilize the communities of Black people for Dr. King to reach. Her vision differed from the male leaders' of that organization, however. She believed that establishing lasting commitment from the people was more important than demonstrations alone.

In 1960 a group of students decided to protest, using nonviolent sit-ins. Their actions motivated other college students to do the same in more than eighty cities, but they struggled to make real impact with their tactics. Ella Baker added fuel to the fires of their movement, branding it under the Student Nonviolent Coordinating Committee (SNCC), where it began to receive national attention. She was the mother of the

American Civil Rights Movement, helping to birth not just these three historic organizations but a code of activism that was selfless and adaptable for future generations. Her goal was to keep the movement about the people and for the people: a movement that didn't depend solely on exceptional individuals to progress. She didn't need the spotlight. Instead of focusing on personal idolization of leaders, she focused on effective change in the most neglected communities.[3]

Ella Baker's impact vibrates through me every time I open my mouth to speak about the modern struggles of Black people. Her importance to the Civil Rights Movement was in all ways equal to that of our great leader Dr. King. However, for a Black woman during that time, the patriarchal hierarchy, even within the Black community, shrank her role in the history books. Her grassroots philosophy and pursuit of justice created a backbone that still carries the movement today.

The contributions of Black women are too often overlooked, but they shaped me. They inspired me. I carry Ella Baker's baton when I march and organize, and it is women like Ida B. Wells and Diane Nash who I think of when I feel like I'm fighting an unfair and unending battle. I carry the obligation of fulfilling these women's legacies, and I take it seriously because I now stand in a place they were never allowed to take, in the forefront.

While the modern movement and my personal ideologies are inspired by Ella Baker, the ways in which we must activate has evolved. Social media has completely changed the game.

Where a message used to take freedom rides and marches to spread across a nation, now it is carried around the world in hours with nothing more than a string of text and a hashtag.

#Blacklivesmatter
#arrestthecops
#trayvonmartin
#sayhername
#georgefloyd
#korryngaines
#philandocastile
#oscargrant
#sandrabland
#freddiegray
#atatianajefferson
#aurarosser
#amadoudiallo
#bothamjean
#altonsterling
#seanbell
#ericgarner
#michaelbrown
#michellecusseaux
#janishafonville
#myahall
#akaigurley
#ahmaudarbery

#rayshardbrooks
#ramarleygraham

With the accessibility to cell phones which have high-quality cameras, everyone can become a reporter in the blink of an eye. Everyone MUST become a reporter when the conditions demand it. It is the responsibility of every single person reading this book to capture misconduct, racism, and brutality when they witness it, especially at the hands of the police. Turning a blind eye is no longer acceptable. Allowing it to take place is the act of a RACIST, and if you're a person of color, your inaction is cowardly. DO SOMETHING. SAY SOMETHING. STAND FOR SOMETHING. Take down names and badge numbers; film harassment, film traffic stops. File a complaint. When you see a Black person interacting with the police, pause your day for just a moment to make sure that things are being handled objectively. I'm not asking you to break any laws or to put yourself in harm's way but to realize that what seems routine to the majority of America can be life-threatening when you are Black or brown. We live in a world where a routine traffic stop can turn into a Black man or woman's last day, in a world where a twelve-year-old child can be shot down for playing with a toy gun.

When we watched George Floyd's eight-minute-and-forty-six-second murder, there was no skewed reporting. There was no right-wing skew. There was no gaslighting to elevate his past crimes above the unrelenting knee to his neck. Social media circulated that video in raw form and forced us to watch a dying man cry for his mother while pleading for his life. It was unfiltered evidence that the true criminal was not the man on the ground but the one wearing a badge. To this day Derek In this distracted world we finally found a way--this time--to hold a policeman to account. It took vivid, brutal pictures and a year of protest, but Chauvin would pay for his crimes. The disgraced officer was convicted for the murder of George Floyd, and on June 25, 2021, he was sentenced to 22.5 years in prison.

Seven
Say All Their Names

ENOUGH IS ENOUGH

While this new wave of social media has inspired a new generation of digital activists, we must remember that reposting, hashtagging, and likes are not enough to provoke real change. We must be more than video activists. Life should matter without having to see it in full color on a cell phone screen. We need a merging of modern tactics with old-school footwork to push legislation and to hold racist cops, institutions, and racist vigilantes accountable for their actions. Social media can help spark a flame, but we need a fire to fix this. Every major movement has that one event, that final straw, that breaks the camel's back.

The final straw for America had a name: Emmett Till. His unjustifiable killing at the hands of a racist mob was the final straw for what we now know as the Civil Rights Movement in America. Emmett Till's murder, committed in response to a white woman's claim that he made an inappropriate sexual advance toward her—

Pause. I will not be another accomplice to that woman's fade into history. I will not gloss over her contribution to the murder of an innocent boy. Justice in the eyes of the law may not have been served for her involvement in the murder of Emmett Till, but in this book, she will be held accountable. Carolyn Bryant told the lie that led to the murder of a fourteen-year-old boy.[1] He was beaten to the point of disfigurement, shot, and tied to a cotton gin before he was thrown into the Tallahatchie River in Money, Mississippi. His murderers were then acquitted. All this brutality. All this evil, commenced over the lie that one white woman told in 1955. It was not the first unjust murder in the Jim Crow South. Black people, Black boys and men, were the victims of lynching, torture, and killing for decades in the South.

The legacy of enslavement hung over the South like a cloud, and although Black people lived freely, if you can call living under Jim Crow and the Ku Klux Klan freedom, the hierarchy and entitlement of power remained. It was not uncommon for white men in white hoods and gowns to pull Black men out of their homes in the middle of the night. Vigilantes exacting punishment, regular citizens acting as judge, jury, and executioner. This was the atmosphere of fear and cruelty that Black people were subjected to.

A TIME TO TAKE SIDES

Emmett Till was the catalyst for what we all call the Civil Rights Movement. Lynchings were, unfortunately, nothing new in 1955, but the brutality of Till's death sparked change. The sacrifice of his life changed the world, changed the law. The "viral" image of Emmett Till's mutilated body, shared with the media by his brave mother, made the offense unmistakable and unforgettable. The Montgomery Bus Boycott went down because Rosa Parks had Emmett Till in the back of her mind as she refused to give up her seat. In much the same way, the brutality of George Floyd's 8:46 was the unignorable catalyst for the most recent uprising. But for me, it started with Amadou Diallo in 1999.

That murder, exceptional for its brutality but not its sentiment, inspired me to fight. Before Amadou Diallo, there were protests and outrage over injustice, but the world hadn't taken notice of the racist spirit pulsing through the American criminal justice system. Then Trayvon Martin happened, and the world took notice, because Trayvon was seventeen years old and his killer was not a cop. George Zimmerman was not protected by the badge. He had not been trained or sworn to duty. He wasn't given a gun by a commanding officer expected to hold him to account. George Zimmerman's command— camouflaged as a volunteer job with his community's neighborhood watch—was to reinforce and act on the sentiment that Black men were dangerous and fit to be exterminated on a whim. Zimmerman's acquittal on all charges related to the shooting seemed to inspire racists everywhere. It felt like every other week, there was a new face of Black extinction on the news. Another murder. Then another. Then another. Mike Brown in St. Louis. Then Philando Castile in Minnesota. Sandra Bland in Texas. The drumbeat of murder was so frequent that America became desensitized to the violence. Even Black America took its eye off the ball. Hashtags and "Rest in Peace" images would go up on social media, but then everyone would move on. I watched this happen again and again. But the emergence of the Black Lives Matter Movement helped prolong the public fight because it gave people language to describe the outrage. That, coupled with the repeated losses of life and the lack of response from our leaders, finally got the ball rolling. People from various organizations organized, we marched, and we went into the community to spur people to demand change. But a start isn't a finish. It isn't progress. It's just that, a start. And in the meantime, our young Black men and boys were still in the crosshairs. So we added new rules to that list of spoken unspoken. Even more sacrifices to the suffocating stench of racism in America. But now the time for respectability politics was over. This was life and death, literally:

Rule #8: No hoodies. Never walk with a garment covering your head.
    Consequence—They will kill you.

Rule #9: No loud music while driving.
    Consequence—They will kill you.

Rule #10: No corner-store runs after dark.
    Consequence—They will kill you.

Rule #11: Don't play with toy guns in the playground.
Consequence—They will kill you.

Rule #12: Never pull a cell phone out of your pocket in view of . . . anyone.
Consequence—They will kill you.

We were adjusting and educating Black boys—and Black girls—on how to avoid being assaulted and murdered because we knew no one else was coming to end the violence on our behalf. That's a backward system. That's a backward solution. Black America has to reprogram the thinking of innocent children to accommodate racist murderers. Come on, America. Come on, humanity. I say again: What the fuck?

Excuse me, but some things demand politically incorrect language. If my choice of vocabulary is what offends you, out of everything I just said, YOU ARE A PART OF THE PROBLEM.

NO JUSTICE, NO PEACE

The sight of murder after murder of unarmed Black men and women created a new level of consciousness. Black people are tired. Every form of peaceful resistance in support of those lost to this sickness has been met with pushback. When Colin Kaepernick knelt, his job was taken from him. Those who followed in Kaepernick's shoes were labeled unpatriotic and punished for it. Nonviolent protests were met with aggressive defenses of the broken status quo. Police hit the streets armed with military gear, rifles, and war tanks. TANKS. Turning military-grade equipment against the citizens who pay for that equipment in the first place is completely unacceptable, but we saw it in cities all across the country with little pushback. The pressure had been rising for years and years, but the catalyst for THIS movement, THIS moment—this best chance to actually change for the better—was one man's suffering. The video that chronicled George Floyd's last moments cut the hearts of all people, regardless of wealth or race. Mothers all over the world heard his cries and reacted with outrage, much like the world reacted to the cries of Mamie Till-Mobley. If social media had existed in 1955, Emmett Till would have been a hashtag too, but we can't allow ourselves to believe that online tribute is a substitute for genuine progress.

When people record the murders of Black people at the hands of police, call that act what it is. Not a tweet, not a viral video, not a TikTok—it's a lynching. In the past, Black children grew up witnessing the bodies of Black men hanging from trees. It was not uncommon to come across their mutilated and charred bodies swinging from branches for the public to see. Black men, often found guilty without trials or representation, were made examples of, and little Black girls and boys took in the message. That's what is happening today when these videos reach altitude online. The more we see the disgraceful images, the more those images incite our resistance. We endured the injustice for a long time, but each time a new Black man or woman is murdered, each time we turn on our news stations and see another report of police brutality, our willingness to *go along to get along* fades. I've seen this firsthand, where members of the Black community who were once muted in this fight, afraid to get their hands dirty, are now reaching the "enough is enough" moment and joining this new movement. The reaction to George Floyd's 8:46 now lives well beyond the murder of one man. George Floyd is the flame that sent our frustrations from a simmer to a rolling boil. All the deaths— the hundreds and thousands of deaths from the slaver's ships, to the plantations, to Jim Crow and the KKK, to George Floyd and Breonna Taylor—it is about all of them. All the lives of the ones we know and don't know, of the names left unsaid, and of the murders left unwitnessed. It is a resistance of the system that allows these things to continue. It's unfortunate that it took such pain and loss to get here, but I am grateful for the cross-cultural alliances that have been formed by our political and social awakening. We will never forget the murder of Breonna Taylor. We will never forget the murder of Ahmaud Arbery. And because of Breonna, the murder of Black women will never go unnoticed and will now be as significant as the murder of Black men.

Eight
No Way Out

THE KNEE ON OUR NECKS

Why is the advancement of people of color so often seen as a threat to the rest of America? It's like white folks are afraid the progress made by Black people will erase the four-hundred-year head start they were given. Quality of life is not an either-or thing. If equality is reached by one race, it doesn't detract from any other community. I just want to make that crystal clear—if Black communities elevate, we aren't going to use that station in society to suppress others from growing or succeeding. The narrative in this country has given the Black community a bad reputation, but we reject being called welfare queens and thugs. Those are labels America branded us with, but that is not who we are at the core. Politicians love to talk about the power of self-reliance when they start their talk about defunding schools and the needy in this country. You'll hear Republicans, primarily (but Democrats aren't immune from this, last names Clinton and Obama included), talking about the power of free markets, entrepreneurship, and hard work to produce freedom for us all. It is my hope that with enough ingenuity and patience, we all will make up for the centuries of inequality that have set the uneven playing field which the babies of Black and brown Americans are born onto every year. That's funny, because history shows that these things—hard work, ingenuity, creativity, and a business-oriented mindset—have rarely, if ever, been allowed to take root in America's marginalized communities. Because whenever Black and brown people have become self-aware enough to see the importance of building out our own economic base, supporting ourselves for our own self-interests, and elevating the discussion around our futures, we've "mysteriously" seen our feet kicked out from under us. Every time a Black organization or community builds power, influence, integrity, and financial governance, white America feels threatened. The consequence is always annihilation. Hence, another rule.

> **Rule #13:** Do not use group economics to rise above the expected status quo.
> *Consequence: They will villainize and destroy the messengers.*

Dr. Martin Luther King, Jr.

We all know who Dr. King is. Everyone reading this book learned about him every February during Black History Month: the father of the Civil Rights Movement and a proponent for nonviolence in his pursuit of justice. Dr. King organized the 1963 March on Washington, spoke before Congress about voting rights and segregation, and led countless demonstrations in the advancement toward freedom for Black people. He was assassinated on April 4, 1968. His family holds firm to this day their belief that the FBI was responsible and that the man convicted of the murder (James Earl Ray) was a fall man.[1]

Malcolm X

Malcolm X was in many ways the counterweight to Dr. King's leadership of the Civil Rights Movement. He represented the more confrontational energy of the cause and was—in his own words—willing to go beyond the simple call for non-violence, believing that racism and white aggression should be fought by "any means necessary." Malcolm X has been both vilified and lionized by history, but here is what is factual: He was a charismatic leader and speaker who grew his influence from Mosque No. 7 in Harlem, New York, as a leader of the Nation of Islam. Not without its own history of controversy, the Nation of Islam grew in strength and influence in the 1950s and 1960s by reflecting the frustrations of Americans who felt left out and left behind by the mainstream Civil Rights Movement. Decades of suffering, death, and despair for Black America had not produced what had been promised. In fact, the record shows that Black and brown influence in government—politicians with voting power—actually *fell* in the time period between Reconstruction and the very recent pre-Obama past. The Nation of Islam was an outgrowth of frustrations, and Malcom X's take-no-prisoners approach reflected those sentiments. He grew the organization by the thousands, developing a loyal following far beyond Harlem and drawing the influential support of people like Muhammad Ali. His name "X" was adopted as a sign of protest against his given slave surname. Malcolm X was well aware of the danger he courted by refusing to take no for an answer to the question of patience in the pursuit of equality; he was well aware that he was being monitored by powerful forces inside and outside of the U.S. government; and he predicted his own early death in the autobiography he elicited *Roots* author Alex Haley to write for him.[2] As was so often the case, Malcolm's analysis proved correct, and he was assassinated on February 21, 1965, in New York City.

The Black Panther Party

The Black Panther Party was founded in 1966 by Huey P. Newton and Bobby Seale in response to police brutality against the African American community. The Black Panthers developed a ten-point program that they expected its members to follow in order to further the economic advancement and protection of Black people. At its height of success, more than two thousand members dedicated themselves to the party's goals to achieve equality for Black people. They were deemed a threat to national security and dismantled by the FBI. Now, I'm not saying the party was perfect or that there weren't issues within its organization, because it is public knowledge that there were. Many of these issues were caused by infiltrators sent by the government to seed division. These same issues exist within every political party humankind had ever known—but it was somehow deemed uniquely unacceptable for the Black Panthers. We Americans watched the Republican Party support Donald Trump, a man who looted our tax dollars for his own private benefit, endangered our own citizens with his negligence around COVID-19, and threatened to destroy the foundations of our democratic systems with conspiracies and violence—where are the calls to shut that party down as a threat to American values? Other political parties are always given a chance to figure themselves out and allowed to exist. The corrupters are weeded out, but the message of the party lives on. The Black Panther Party, on the other hand, was extinguished entirely because it represented the interests of Black people as it accrued power.[3]

Rosewood

Rosewood was a small, prosperous Black community in Florida that was terrorized by white men and burned to the ground in 1923. Black men—everyday business owners, artists, engineers and entrepreneurs—were lynched for daring to prosper outside the lines of white supremacy. Their ears and fingers were cut off as trophies while their bodies swung from trees. Women were kidnapped and raped. Children were forced to watch their parents be slaughtered and then murdered beside them. Government officials had knowledge that terror—in any other context, a race riot—was taking place, but they did nothing to stop it. Survivors and descendants of the massacre's victims were given $150,000 in 1994, seventy-one years after the horrific events took place.[4] It was a form of reparations (although the government wouldn't dare call it that) rarely afforded to injured Americans.

Black Wall Street

The Greenwood District of Tulsa, Oklahoma, was the most affluent Black neighborhood of the twentieth century. It was a self-sufficient region where Blacks had established wealth and ownership from 1906 until 1921. Railroad tracks separated Blacks and whites, allowing a fully realized Black economy to flourish. Black entrepreneurs and professionals flocked to the region, amassing wealth and independence never seen in this country before or since. It was Black excellence on its own terms. Many Black families lived better than the white folks on the other side of the tracks, making the community a target of simmering animosity. It's been said the Black dollar was recycled within Greenwood nineteen times,[5] helping the economy to grow and keeping Black businesses open. The neighborhood had its own bank, post office, nightclubs, theaters, and doctors' offices. It even had its own Black newspaper. It was the mecca of Black wealth during a time of racial divide in this country. It was a place where Black people could shake the history of slavery and begin to change the trajectory for future generations. Wealth, Black wealth, was built there, earning the district the nickname "Black Wall Street." In a racially divided and violent period in America, Greenwood's white neighbors felt that Black people had no business obtaining that type of luxury and wealth. This should sound familiar: The IDEA of Black freedom, lived without sufficient fear and limitation, was treated as a criminal act. All it took was for a seventeen-year-old white girl to accuse a nineteen-year-old Black boy, by the name of Dick Rowland, of sexual assault for racist white supremacists to do what they had been waiting to do all along.[6] Fifteen hundred white men lined up outside the courthouse with the intention to lynch Dick Rowland. When they clashed with a group of Black members of the community, the massacre began. Mobs of white people, supported by the National Guard, terrorized the Greenwood community. As many as three hundred people were killed, and the entire neighborhood was burned to the ground.[7] Their only crime was being Black, wealthy, and free.

Elaine Massacre

In 1919 sharecroppers in Elaine, Arkansas, gathered to discuss fair wages and organizing with the Progressive Farmers and Households Union.[8] Membership in the union would help Black sharecroppers negotiate a better price for the cotton they picked and sold to white farmers. When a group of white men received word of the meeting, they went to the church, instigating conflict by shooting into what they believed to be an ongoing meeting. The sharecroppers returned fire, resulting in the death of one white man. Rumors of an insurrection spread like wildfire, and more than one thousand white vigilantes confronted the Black citizens of Elaine. A race riot ripped through the Black community, leaving behind the bodies of men, women, and children. You would think that law enforcement would step in to stop the madness, but instead, police assisted in the slaughter. Even the governor sent troops in with orders to kill. Armed with machine guns, they slaughtered more than two hundred Blacks, some with guns, others hanged, and many more tortured and burned alive inside their homes. The madness lasted for five days.

Philadelphia Move
In May 1985, Osage Avenue in Philadelphia, Pennsylvania, was occupied by a communal group of Black freedom fighters called MOVE.[9] They were anti-establishment, anti-institution, and believed in relying on a holistic, natural, agricultural, and hunter-gatherer way of life. Today they might get a hashtag, a YouTube channel, and a cookbook series. The group opposed modern technology and medicine. In their community, they often organized movements against institutions that supported enslavement of life in all forms, including prisons, zoos, and circuses. They believed all living beings had the right to freedom and movement. Let there be no misunderstanding—they were loud. They disrupted, and it caused tension between

MOVE members and local police. They wore their hair in locs, and each member took on the surname "Africa." Their way of living and habit of both conducting and attracting protests within the neighborhood caused a disturbance. But violence was never their tactic of choice. Nonetheless, locals complained, arrest warrants were issued, and Philadelphia police launched a siege against MOVE's headquarters. The two sides, police and inhabitants, exchanged fire. One officer was killed and sixteen others, including police and firefighters, were injured in the melee. Nine MOVE members were charged in the officer's death, and tensions between the group and the police continued to escalate. Locals were no more tolerant of their peculiar ways, but again—this MOVE was far from violent. Regardless, Mayor Wilson Goode and Police Commissioner Gregore Sambor declared them a terrorist organization, opening the door to their next play. In May 1985 Philadelphia police launched another attack on MOVE's compound, now with almost five hundred officers. A gunfight broke out, and Philadelphia bombed the MOVE compound as a tactic to force its members out. The resulting fire spread to sixty-one homes and claimed eleven lives of members of the organization, five of them children. When given the opportunity to contain the fire, police officials made the decision to let it burn, to eradicate the "problem" for good. The area has never recovered. The green light to bomb a city block in a white neighborhood would never be permitted.

DIE OR LIVE FREE

Black America just wants to exist. To live peacefully without fear of being condemned for that which we can't control: our skin color. All the movements I discussed here were threats to the establishment because, in this society, any form of Black power is seen as inherently dangerous. We, the disempowered, do not desire to dominate. I certainly do not, and none of the leaders I organize with or on behalf of wish to take anything away from others in order to build ourselves up. Equitable solutions, solutions that share and ensure *opportunity,* do not take away. No one loses in a society that is fair. There should be no fear of freeing our vulnerable from the expectation of violence and dismissal. I am almost impressed by the number of ways in which these ideas about equity have been spun and mischaracterized to make the average person—in America, the "average" is a white woman in her late thirties[10]—feel personally attacked, somehow personally put at risk, by an "other" who holds no formal power. It's crazy.

While these people and movements were not without controversy, the most important connecting factor was their love for Black folks and their motivation to organize in opposition to forces of inequity. America will tolerate Black health crises, Black poverty, Black illness, and Black dysfunction. The things this country has always refused to tolerate is Black equity and self-determination.

Massacres led by racists and anarchists have plagued the

Black community for centuries, but the new movement led by millennials and Gen Z, the fresh faces who have accepted the baton from elders of the Civil Rights Movement, they AIN'T HAVING IT. They match the energy being served by the system. Going along to get along is not enough. Working penny-ante jobs and being undereducated and set aside AREN'T OPTIONS. Attempts to terrorize and intimidate DO NOT FAZE these young people. Being out there with this younger generation makes me more courageous.

The millennial activist and the Gen Z activist have a different threshold for tolerance. So the unmovable goals are justice and equity. We are far removed from the inherited fear that the Jim Crow South utilized to keep the Black community in line. No form of pushback, no legislation, no intimidation is large enough to deter us from pursuing righteousness. The biggest opponent we face, ironically, is the very institution we're supposed to call for help.

THE POLICE.

WHERE WE'RE GOING

Nine
Defund the Police

THE $100 BILLION MONEY PIT

Society accepts the narrative that Black men are dangerous thugs who run in gangs and terrorize communities with guns and drugs, but I've never encountered a single Black man who frightens me as much as the police. For Black people in America, the police are the gangs. Too many of us simply do not call the police for anything, ever. It's no exaggeration.

Rule #14: Do not call the police.
Consequence: They will escalate the conflict.

A hundred billion dollars. That's how much America spends to fund police departments annually. It would cost a fraction of that—$216 million—to fix Flint's water crisis.[1] The city of Baltimore needs $823 million to improve its public school system.[2] Eliminating college tuition would cost $79 billion per year.[3] But instead of financing any of these things that would instantly improve the quality of life in this country, we pour the money into police departments. Money is stockpiled into one sector of American communities while so many failing or nonexistent programs go without basic support. Police budgets constitute 20 to 50 percent of the general budget of cities across the nation.[4] Social services go unfunded or underfunded, children attend schools struggling with pest infestations and leaky roofs, and public housing continues to fall apart. But through it all, those operating behind a badge are rarely if ever asked to account for their budgets. You would think this money glut would result in a professional, well-behaved workforce, but time and again, incidents of escalation, mistreatment, and bigotry show that police departments still have a lot of work to do. Instead of creating new programming or putting city budgets to work to directly tackle challenges like homelessness, health care, and education, taxpayer dollars have been wasted to turn police forces into a militarized public enemy. Inner-city neighborhoods don't need more tanks, more drones, and more cops on the street. We need more solutions to real problems that don't fit inside the easy box of punishable crime. We need our starving babies fed. We need boys with minds for scholarship to be given books instead of guns. We need clean water in our homes. We need grocery stores in our neighborhoods and access to loans for our businesses. We need opportunities to occupy space beyond graves and prisons. Yet America remains determined to pave those paths for Black America.

Too often police represent the opposite of safety in our communities. We have not been given reason to trust them. We need access to resources that present other options to empower and build safer communities. We also need alternatives to incarceration based in care and frameworks like transformative justice, not punishment. Punishment has not made our hoods safe, and the idea that we're X number of arrests away from punishing ourselves into safety is ridiculous. We want safe and accountable communities, but in order to get there, we need assurances that all of our people will have their basic needs met, the resources to thrive, and a nonpunitive means of response to violence, conflict, and harm within our communities. Give us a chance to save ourselves by redistributing wealth from the criminal sectors of our neighborhoods to the areas where our resources are lacking.

Misguided readings of history have shaped a society where an overseer seems necessary. The institutional design of policing we wrestle with today is still too closely modeled after a past where society employed bands of white gangs to catch slaves on behalf of wealthy landowners. Where informal police forces were brought in to maintain order among newly freed slaves, and to protect property. It's how white America was trained to be more enraged by burning buildings than the Black man on the ground with the knee to his neck. The conception of a society where brutal police power doesn't exist is so foreign to American minds that we can't even begin to discuss the alternatives in polite tones. The institution of law enforcement, as we understand it here and now, is a remnant of our four-hundred-year tradition of enslavement.

Of institutional power. Of catching and killing. It is a decaying model that must change. The rest of the world has already started this work of prioritizing wellness and the well-being of human consciousness over pure displays of violence and power.

Elsewhere in society—outside the prisons and off the police details—we see mental health emerging as a top priority of any modern, caring civilization. Discussions of mental wellness, or the lack thereof, are being held on the job, in schools, and among people young and old as we realize that a life where we do not care for and respect one another is not a life being lived freely. In short, people have their shit: their mental and emotional weights that color the ways in which they interact with the rest of the world. How is it that this notion has not changed the way we police our society? How is it that we consider the mental wellness of every person except those living in our most distressed communities? We have undergone a shift in our thinking globally in every sector except policing. Not every 911 requires that an armed enforcer pull onto the scene. The number-one reason Black people fear the police is because the current style of policing comes with the intent to do harm instead of to help. Officers are trained to expect— and therefore invite—confrontation with the communities they serve. Arrests and detainment are not viewed with the weight and respect they demand; these acts of authority and aggression are not to be taken lightly, yet we get lulled to sleep with brands like "stop and frisk," as if having one's freedom taken away at the threat of personal harm becomes routine so long as it is temporary. Don't get me wrong, there are a number of officers who go to work every day truly wanting to keep everyone safe. The issue is not with individual officers. It is a systemic problem that persists no matter the diverse feelings of individual cops.

Police officers, often male and white,[5] are called into urban neighborhoods that they do not care about or hold any personal relationships in. They enter as a mercenary force employed to maintain order, not protect peace. They enter Black communities with biased expectations of the habits and behaviors of Black people and react out of fear instead of with knowledge. But we can also see that Black and other officers of color engage in similar varieties of biased police violence.[6] The problem isn't the race or background of the police officers, it's the policing itself. If public safety were community-based, we might see violence interveners or conflict resolution teams walking the same beat, unarmed, getting to know the happenings of the people they serve and able to distinguish between the mentally ill homeless veteran and the criminal doing harm. Police—with their automatic assault rifles, their bulletproof vests, their helmets, their shields, and their batons—show up armed to fight a war when sometimes all that is needed is a liaison who can facilitate treatment and instill order in a chaotic situation.

The solution is simple. We must, yes, *DEFUND* THE POLICE and refund our communities. Now, let me stop you right here, because I can practically hear your eyes bulging at this thought. Nobody is saying that people should not have entities to call when they're in harm's way, but we need to dismantle policing and surveillance as they currently exist and build new models of safety. People should have options to call upon various kinds of safety intervention, not just one model centered around a badge, a gun, and a license to kill. Take domestic violence, for example. Estimates suggest that 40 percent of police households experience domestic violence[7]—yet the only option many people have to call when they experience domestic violence is that very same community struggling with its own handling of the issue. We need an overhaul of public safety. And that needs to include centering frameworks like transformative justice that center care, not punishment, vengeance, and control.[8]

Liquidating the excessive funds that keep armed police forces in a position of unmatched authority will create the opportunity to distribute resources in other areas of importance. Instead of having one overburdened entity, the money used to finance police operations would instead be spread around to create infrastructure that decreases the need for a militarized police presence:

Mental health services
Drug treatment programs
Affordable and quality housing
Job placement
Universal basic income
Social work

Quality education
Summer jobs and after-school programs for youth
Universal health care

In a community where these social programs and resources thrive, violence and harm decrease. Disenfranchised communities of Black and brown people have endured a lack of funding for generations. The only entity within those communities that is funded is the very one we have been conditioned not to trust: the police.

The systems currently in place are built around the idea of consequence instead of community. When a mother can't feed her children, they are taken away and put into foster care. When a man can't afford housing for his family, they are evicted and forced to figure it out on the streets. When the elderly or ailing can't afford medication, they are left to fend for themselves, often turning to illegal means of self-medication. There is no attempt to fix the problem, only punishment of the afflicted. That results in further alienation, which only inflames tensions because the police are the representatives of the institution . . . they are the physical representation of the law.

Children can't call 911 when they're hungry or when the cold of winter creeps through subsidized housing that is barely standing and overrun with rodents. Mentally ill men and women who are self-medicating with street drugs because they can't afford to see real doctors can't plead their cases when the police mistake them for suspects. Armed police can't provide undereducated mothers with job skills and accreditation that would help them provide for their families.

It feels as if there is no end to the list of abuses America is willing to let simmer for hundreds of years, not caring so long as they don't spill into the comfortable existence of affluent suburban life. But the irrationality of that equation is most evident in policing—where infinite resources are applied to address easily defined problems. More, more heavily armed, and more expensive police are not the answer to America's fear of its impoverished and segregated communities. Defunding and reallocating resources are vital. That is what we mean when we say DEFUND. It is not an overnight abandonment of security and law. It is a deeper consideration of how we *choose* to address society's problems.

When you give people something to live for and they can take pride in the place they call home, the upkeep of the community will come from the members who benefit from the resources. We need to transform how we approach public safety at all levels. We need divest/invest campaigns and demands for resource reallocation to continue growing across the country. At the federal and state level, the Movement for Black Lives's BREATHE Act provides model legislation for divesting from policing and systems of punishment and funding our communities.[9] The burden of policing inner-city neighborhoods decreases when society invests in its healing. But that doesn't mean things might not happen, and for that, we will still need alternative crisis and emergency response systems.[10]

The units and officers who police inner-city, predominately Black neighborhoods are designed to target Black people and arrest. Their purpose is to keep order, but the intimidating presence causes disorder. The police determine lawfulness in inner-city areas based on skin color, not suspicion. This is predatory and gives the police justification to approach any Black man or woman without cause. It results in harassment. Something we don't talk about enough is the fact that the second most common report of police misconduct is sexual violence, which disproportionately impacts Black women.[11]

I see it every day, any time I climb into the car with a Black man. Even driving is a suspicious act when performed while Black. Without breaking any law, Black men are pulled over, and traffic stops involving Black men aren't like your average traffic stop. The predatory position that police officers take over Black people during traffic stops has gotten many people killed. In milder cases, officers use it as cause to do illegal searches of vehicles, to pull Black citizens from their cars, and to humiliate innocent men and women by violently cuffing them in public and by pulling apart their personal property. It is a level of disrespect that no other group of people is constantly subjected to. A simple traffic stop of an unarmed person should never end in injury, death, or a complete civil rights violation, but it often does for Black people in America. It is terrifying to interact with the police. Being innocent and Black is worse than being guilty and white in this country. The police behave as adversaries rather than community allies.

The remedy is to remove the threat of biased enforcement through the efforts of community governance. Creating crisis management programs, then putting qualified people from the community within these systems to combat nonviolent crises, helps rehabilitate the infrastructure inside urban areas. Erica Ford and A. T. Mitchell, who designed the New York Crisis Management System, have a proven model that curbs violent as well as nonviolent issues. The holistic community-based models are at the core of their violence prevention research.

To grow up in a decaying neighborhood and then contribute to its healing injects pride and ownership into a community. Community advocates called out in instances of mental health emergencies, domestic affairs, and social service crises can be much more effective than relying on armed police officers, whose main aim is to enforce law. Law is not always the answer. Plenty of laws have been created to the detriment of the powerless for the benefit of the powerful. Laws and morality aren't always the same thing. It used to be legal to own human beings. So, no, enforcement of the law is not necessarily the solution. Sometimes all it takes is love from people within the community, people who understand a community's issues, and resources provided to give a community the chance to fix itself.

We have yet to attempt this at the scale it needs in order to be done. Police department budgets continue to swell, even as the excesses of law enforcement become more and more evident. I look forward to a world where the gun pointed at the little Black boy instead becomes a hand extended, where the intent to harm becomes the intent to help, and where the fear of people we don't understand is replaced with faith in humanity. Black people need safety, but police and prisons are not the answer. The blatant disrespect and disparity of treatment when interacting with Black men and women are disgusting. We still live in a country where Dylann Roof can kill nine Black people in a church yet be apprehended peacefully, but a Black man selling cigarettes on a street corner is put in a chokehold until all life is squeezed from his body. The aggression toward Black citizens who pose no threat is an everyday story playing in national news. We will not accept this. This is acceptable only to people who subscribe to white-supremacy ideals. The Racists versus the Anti-racists. The people who stand with me, beside me, the people reading this book to figure out how we got here and where we go from this dark place . . . we demand transformation. Communities must govern over themselves in a way that makes them proud of the communities they are developing. When the people have a say in the programming that is created to help self-sustain, they will utilize the programming proudly. But the community's voice must be loud in order to be recognized, and the only ways to let the institution know we have something to say are to organize, to unify, and to PROTEST.

Ten

Harnessing the Power of Our Voice

WHAT IT MEANS TO BE A PROTESTER

Protesting, marching, and occupying are the most effective ways to bring attention to our issues. I am an experienced protester. I've walked over two hundred miles, from New York to Washington, DC, to bring awareness to criminal justice issues. I've been flash-bombed by police on the streets of Louisville, Kentucky. I've been tear-gassed in Minneapolis. I am prepared for the sometimes dangerous encounters I experience when I decide to march in the name of justice for my community.

We all inherently understand that there is a strength in numbers, yet one of the greatest challenges of resistance organizing is to convince the individual that his/her voice is important enough to contribute to the collective. Activists are inspired by either an injustice they've experienced personally or an injustice they've witnessed that is so grave that doing nothing feels wrong.

The right to protest is taken as sacred in America, but sacred should not be confused for easy. Anyone can show up to a protest, but it is critical that the rules of protest not be lost in your passion to take part in change. In my advocacy for freedom, I often give up my own. I can't even count all the times I've been arrested, but I made the decision that my personal liberties aren't as important as the greater mission of my cause. The school of activism that I follow—the one Ella Baker started—is the community approach. Many are enraged about the state we're living in, but few know what to do to help change things. Yet you're doing it right now. It starts here. You're informing yourself on the moment and how the past culminated to the racial tension that has boiled over today, but most important, you're taking action to help remedy what is to come. But if you're going to be out here, advocating, allying, and representing the movement, you must know the rules of engagement.

GUIDELINES FOR ALLYSHIP

1. Ask yourself: Who is calling the protest?

Who are you following? Don't blindly engage in a movement that you know nothing about. Does the ideology of leadership align with your own? You don't have to agree with every single stance taken by an organization or social justice figure, but your overall moral code should align. Once you choose a side and become a contributor to a cause, you take on the identity of the brand. Make sure it's one you will be proud to be a part of.

Complete a safety check for yourself! Anything can happen during a protest. Literally anything. Just because you go into a protest with the intention of being peaceful doesn't mean it will remain that way. Have a plan to account for your own well-being. Give someone you trust the information about the efforts you will be participating in. Have an emergency contact in place and know that phone number by heart. Some even take the precaution of writing an emergency contact number on their body before taking to the field. If you get arrested or if you are injured, cell phones and bags may get lost, but a phone number written on your forearm is accessible to both you and anyone coming to your aid.

2. Keep it light.

Keep the number of materials being carried on your person to a minimum. Protests are long and exhausting. You're on your feet for hours at a time, sometimes even entire days. You will need your hands. Keep them free of unnecessary baggage.

3. Always keep your identification on you.

Know where it is. Do not lose it. The last thing you want is to be stopped, questioned, or arrested without a proper way of identifying who you are. That is just the kind of excuse an unethical actor looks for to deny citizens their rights to protest and assembly. Have an ID accessible in a place that doesn't require you to reach for it. The goal is to make it home at the end of the night, not to become another victim of police brutality. Make sure they can identify you formally IF the situation arises.

4. Research the issue.

Not only should you know *who* you're following, but you should know the message. The media is always present during a protest. If you happen to find yourself being interviewed, you want to be able to speak to the framework of why you are there. Passion is good, it's key to a protest, but knowledge supporting that passion is even better. A combination of the two is effective, and as participants to a movement, we must always be effective. The last thing you want to do is speak publicly about an organization and misinform or serve as a distraction due to a lack of knowledge, so prepare beforehand.

5. Have a bail fund and a bailout person handy.

Again, know these resources by heart or write them down on your body. DO NOT ASSUME THAT YOU WILL MAKE IT HOME. This is a different day and era for activists. You can be doing everything by the book and still become a target. I've seen plenty of nonviolent protesters arrested and charged with felonies for no reason at all. Be prepared for the possibility.

Following these rules can mean life or death. Protesting isn't a fad. It isn't something to engage in for social media likes. It is serious business. For those of us who walk this path of freedom fighting, it's life-threatening. I work very hard to stay safe and keep my people safe with me. This work is not all glory, and there are more losses than wins. I risk my life every day I choose to speak out against injustice, but this is what God called me to do. I didn't choose this fight, this fight chose me, but I engage responsibly. I follow these rules to ensure the safety of myself and my team. If you are going to join any movement, I urge you to keep them in mind as well.

There are safer and less safe ways to protest, but there is no right or wrong way to combat injustice. Protest can come in the form of one person using his/her/their voice to advocate for a cause, or many people coming together to magnify a message. Most important, from my perspective, when we talk about "right" or "wrong" ways to protest, is how our actions serve the intent of the demonstration. How do we approach the mission and make sure it gains the productive attention it deserves with a reaction that helps push forward the needle of equality? Movements gain traction when an event occurs that stimulates the moral obligation of not just one group of people but all people.

DECENTRALIZED ORGANIZING

Activism after the killing of George Floyd started with decentralized demonstrations in and around the Minneapolis site of his death but quickly spread worldwide. Decentralized protests don't always have a leader. There is no one face to the movement and often no plan for an official organization. Decentralized protests often capture and reflect the highly charged nature of the moment. They often include reactions of pain, rage, and impulsivity. These demonstrations are grassroots efforts, often springing up impromptu. Older leaders from the civil rights era would call this form of protesting counterproductive because it comes with a number of potential pitfalls:

- There are no formal demands.
- There is no identifiable leadership.
- The message can easily become confused.
- There are no clearly defined codes of conduct.
- It takes a lot to maintain focus.
- Mixed messages can damage the overall purpose.

In my experience, the decentralized movement is tricky, but it can also be very effective because it is unpredictable to the authorities. An uncontrolled movement is more threatening to its targets because the institution knows no one leader can sway its actions. It is difficult for the oppressor to offer "clout" or access to one person in exchange for watering down the tone of the movement. Its motivating fuel is anger.

"A riot is the language of the unheard," Dr. Martin Luther King, Jr., once said. Black people have been dying at the hands of racists for generations. We've been praying for change for just as long. We've been crying over murdered sons for longer. Been marching. Been kneeling. Been singing. Been hoping. Been pleading.

Yet we are still unheard.

Decentralized protests do not always escalate, but when they do, the frustrations of the people sometimes lead to destruction. When cities go up in flames. When big retail stores burn. When businesses are looted. When windows are broken. When police cars are flipped, some clarity is lost around what is and is not acceptable in response to outrage. I don't agree with violent actions, but I do understand when frustrations boil over because we've been screaming, and we've been ignored. Our elders marched until their bones could no longer carry the weight of injustice. Some of the folks in our movement have stopped believing in the nonviolent strategy I preach. In order to avoid more violent outbursts, there needs to be swift accountability by our justice system when innocent Black citizens are murdered.

In the words of many and all who fight for fairness:

"If we don't get no justice, there ain't gonna be no peace."

Target, Walmart, AutoZone don't get to come into the inner-city neighborhoods, earn inner-city patronage, inner-city dollars, and say nothing when Black people are murdered. The NFL doesn't get to make money off Black athletes and do nothing when unarmed Black men are shot dead. White-owned corporations don't get to profit off our dollars and be silent when we are killed. This fight isn't one that can be won without allies, and allies are not silent in the face of inhumanity. Allies speak up, allies are clear on where they stand. And an ally must stand with us, next to us, not at a convenient distance.

When the goals of corporate business place profit over justice and suck resources out of our communities without pouring anything back in, they become a target of rage. Many don't understand how some Black folks are okay with burning the communities they live in. The systems of disenfranchisement and wealth accumulation we operate under in America mean that Black people often have no stake in the physical manifestations of their communities. Most inner-city Black neighborhoods are filled with renters. Those who do own their home and land are often bought out for cheap so that corporate companies can build and restore neighborhoods, not for the Black people who exist there but for white families who come in and push the existing homeowners out. We call that gentrification. You can't take pride in something that isn't yours, and only 44 percent of Black people own homes in America.[1] Even fewer own commercial properties. Especially in high-rent urban districts, many Black business owners have paid rent long enough to purchase the site of their company many times over. But the racist nature of finance in America often sees Black and brown people denied financing from banks to make those kinds of financial decisions. This leaves Black people permanent renters on city blocks where they have lived their entire life. While the emotional ownership in these neighborhoods is high, physical ownership doesn't exist—so maybe it should not be shocking when frustrations turn to property damage in conditions where words have gone ignored for far too long.

This is one of the by-products of decentralized protesting. It's not always pretty, and it's not always safe, but it does force people to pay attention. It's the last resort on a very long list of ways a frustrated and ignored group of people have tried in their calls for help. Those fires aren't started for nothing. They are flare guns in the darkness. They are calls for help.

Sometimes the violence is ignited by detractors of the movement who want to muddy the message and make the protest appear unstable, and because of the hopelessness of some of the people, folks latch on and engage in the distractions. It has been my mission to keep people focused in those moments.

CENTRALIZED ORGANIZING

Centralized organizing is a form of activism with a more traditional design. It has a brand behind it: a leader even disinterested people feel they can listen to, a leader who gives direction and a strict narrative to demonstrations. It is organized from the top, and the message trickles down to participants who are allies with the fight for freedom and equality.

Often organized protesters follow a code of conduct. An example would be the Greensboro Sit-ins of 1960, when members of the Student Nonviolent Coordinating Committee occupied white establishments and, to protest segregation in the Jim Crow south, refused to leave.[2] It was highly coordinated. It took extreme discipline. Starting with four students who subscribed to Dr. King's nonviolent approach, they occupied space at F. W. Woolworth's lunch counter during a time of segregation in the South. They were asked to leave but refused, sitting nonviolently. The white regulars harassed these students, threatening them, calling in bomb threats, bringing out the Ku Klux Klan, but the students didn't move. Those students returned every day, attracting more and more attention, gaining more allies with every sit-in, eventually spreading the movement to fifty-five cities in thirteen states. It made the nation take heed. It was a pivotal contribution to the civil rights era and helped end segregation.

Centralized protesting is a way to make clear the demands of the movement. Under a brand, there is a safety net that leaves one face in the forefront to take the hits that come along with leadership. Until Freedom is the umbrella under which I activate. We are a hybrid of centralized and decentralized organizing. Our mission is to figure out how to utilize the benefits of both strategies to effect change. Leadership is diverse within my organization. We don't have one leader. We have many. We don't throw away the foundation that our elders have laid for us. We stand on it, we stand on their shoulders, but today the movement has space for diversity in leadership. We have men, Black people, political folks, folks who've been in the criminal-legal system, violence prevention folks. The current movement is one where all perspectives are needed and uplifted. The issues are diverse, so the voices carrying the message must be diverse. It's the unity that allows us to cover the entire Black experience. While some call me the voice of this movement, I am merely an amplifier of many. I am not *the* leader of this movement. I am a contributor to it. We are a family, moving as a unit to accomplish the goal of true freedom. I say "true" because America has a way of giving a little only to come back and take a lot. Emancipate us with forty acres and a mule only to take it back. Give us government assistance only to take the patriarchs of our household. Give us the illusion of freedom only to hold our civil liberties hostage. Take our sons. Kill our leaders. Gentrify our neighborhoods.

AMERICA TAUGHT US HOW TO LOOT!
AMERICA TAUGHT US VIOLENCE.
AMERICA MOLDED THE BLACK COMMUNITY.
WE LEARNED THIS FROM YOU!

Whether we choose to protest in peace or in uproar, the choice is ours, because it is American history that tells us violence is the method. Deviations from destruction come from self-restraint, not any examples set out by those who have carried out the subjugation of our Black and brown citizens. We never owned the hoses, the batons, or the dogs that disrupted non-violent protests. Those were not Black and brown faces under the white hoods that strung men and boys from trees, left burning crosses in our yards, and bombed little girls in churches. While Dr. Martin Luther King, Jr., taught a generation to be nonviolent, America was using violence to intimidate. So when pain spills onto the streets and buildings burn, the example being followed is not one set by those lighting the flames. What's the solution? Set a new example. Initiate change.

Whether a protest is planned or spur-of-the-moment, there will always be something that goes wrong. No matter how righteous a cause may be or how necessary the movement is, there is always the presence of the other side. The objectors. The detractors. The white-supremacy groups. The privileged folks who are so far removed from the problem, they can't see that racism exists at an institutional level, not just between individuals. The media. The police. There are so many opponents when you are out there on the front lines, and it can be intimidating. It can be confusing. Separating true protesters from usurpers of the message is important. I've been in the middle of city blocks mid-protest and I have witnessed white men show up to disturb nonviolent demonstrations. White supremacists and anti-fascist groups have often been the cause of looting in this modern wave of protest. They come and they vandalize buildings, they set fires, they place bricks in the middle of peaceful organizers in hopes of inciting violence.

Why? Violence detracts from the fluency of the message. If protesters against police brutality and racism are gathered nonviolently, our message is crystal clear. Creating chaos helps to paint the image that Black communities are filled with thugs and that our streets are corrupt with danger. When outside members of a neighborhood come into our protests to wreak havoc, they intend to muddle our voices. This tactic will incite a reaction from a new protester, but it is the experienced protester who recognizes the ulterior motive and remains in control of the movement. I've learned over time that discipline and self-control are imperative in activism. Mastering those things has kept me alive in many circumstances. During my residency in Louisville as I was organizing and advocating for Breonna, we were met with resistance, and when I say "resistance," I mean exactly that. White militia groups don't come quietly. They come armed with assault rifles, military gear, Confederate flags, army fatigues, and hate as fuel to counter our efforts. They block off city blocks, creating traps for protesters. While nonviolent protesters of the movement were harassed in Louisville and arrested for occupying the streets, the white militia went unchecked.

I witnessed what seemed to be an unspoken alliance between local law enforcement and these hate groups: They were allowed to assemble. The cops never acted against them, never dismantled their groups, never asked them to get off the streets. It seemed the curfew was in place only for certain types of people. This type of energy, amid a situation where emotions are already running high, is antagonizing. It's natural to feel anger and want to react, but the best thing to do is nothing. A reaction is what hate groups want. I have learned not to engage under any circumstance because the media won't see the instigation, they will only measure the reaction, and the wrong reaction from protesters destroys the legitimacy of the protest. It's why centralized protesting can be so effective, because before anyone hits the streets, a code of conduct and direction is established. You know the rules of engagement beforehand because they have been clearly defined by the top organizers.

Protesting with allies from other communities is helpful because it magnifies the message. Unity is always the goal, but guests of the community must come into the movement with the motivation to be helpful, not harmful. I've seen non-violent protests erupt when white college students come into town under the guise of protesting but are there to turn up. It feels like a thrill to the privileged to come to the hood and be among the masses. It's loud. It's crowded. It's dangerous. It must feel like a field trip to the ghetto to some, but at the end of the night, when everything is destroyed, those white faces get to go home. The people who live in these neighborhoods are left to endure the destruction caused by others. It's one thing for the residents of a community to be fueled by pain, but for outsiders to take advantage of that pain and tear up our neighborhoods for sport is a mockery of the movement. This is also a form of detraction. Any person who weakens the cause and turns the focus to violence instead of peace is an enemy to equality. We are not out here for fun. We are not marching for entertainment.

The difference between Black protesters and allies of the movement is that allies of the movement march because they *want to*. Black people march because we HAVE TO. If we don't march, we bury our sons. If we don't use our voice, one day a cop pulls us over and our heart stops in fear because we aren't sure if we'll make it through a traffic ticket with our life.

Even protesters from within the community must check their rage at times. While I do understand that emotions run high, it can be counterproductive in the grand scheme of things to let violence overrun the protest. Antagonists, provoking reactions from the police, your passion lacking direction, all those things devalue the message. We must always remember the elders, the children, and the vulnerable who are out there with us. DO NOT USE THE COVER OF A PROTEST AS A MEANS TO GET YOUR PERSONAL REPARATIONS.

A freedom fighter must be self-disciplined enough not to engage when provoked and to stay the course without becoming distracted by opposers in the moment. We must act together and streamline our wants, following a code of conduct that allows our voices to be amplified so that the media doesn't build a case against the cause for the irresponsible choices of a few. Every protest will have some people who use the moment incorrectly, but it shouldn't be those with interest in using protest for progress.

Eleven

Other Strategies for Change

SPEAK WITH YOUR WALLET

One of the most successful and admirable protests in American history was the organizing of the Montgomery Bus Boycotts. When I assemble my own family of freedom fighters, I look to this movement as the example of what effective centralized protesting can accomplish. On December 1, 1955, in Montgomery, Alabama, Rosa Parks refused to give up her seat to a white passenger. Only a hundred days after Emmett Till was killed, Blacks in the Jim Crow South were fed up with the cruel and unequal treatment. Injustice after injustice piled on top of the Black community, and Rosa Parks's arrest was the final straw. Blacks in Montgomery, Alabama, organized their efforts, deciding to boycott the bus system altogether. They spread the message of the protests through church ministries and grass-roots newspapers. It's estimated that forty thousand Black bus riders boycotted the Alabama bus system.[1] For over a year, the boycott remained in place, crippling the public transit system. The brilliance behind this movement was the commitment.

I organize on the ground every day, and I can attest it is difficult to get thousands of people to stay the course and trust the leadership to execute the vision of the people. Often exhaustion, fear, and hopelessness can tire protesters into abandoning the mission. When it seems like nothing is being done and that society has given us as much as we're going to get, it's easy to accept the status quo. The strategic planning that leaders like Dr. Martin Luther King, Jr., and John Lewis implemented to make sure the community could endure the boycott was the key to its success. They created a symbolic picket line, and no one crossed it. Black taxi drivers and carpooling became common modes of transportation. Those who had no access to cars opted to walk before supporting the racist and segregated bus system. Three hundred and eighty-one days of this led to a major win in the fight for civil rights in America. No one person was powerful enough to make the stride in history. Protesting isn't about one individual. It's about a bunch of individuals uniting under one idea to amplify the message.

This boycott had a clear purpose from the very beginning and had visible leadership who reiterated the importance of staying the course. The people believed in both the cause and those who led from the front. They held the line, connecting the element of protesting to the economic welfare of the system. They messed with the system's ability to profit. Taking away the Black dollar proved how much the Black dollar was needed in Alabama. It is a strategy that has been attempted many times, but I've never seen it accomplished as well as during the Montgomery Bus Boycott. It was one of the most successful mass demonstrations by and for Black people in America. Imagine if we organized in this way today. Black people spend over $1 trillion a year in the United States.[2] What those forty thousand Black men and women did was demand respect and equal treatment for their hard-earned money. They refused to be treated like second-class citizens while funding white systems. The hardship of the protests didn't deter them from sustaining. There is a lesson to be learned from history. One thing that all people understand is the power of money. If disenfranchised communities who have been disregarded and taken advantage of would stand against companies known for discrimination and racism, we would gain leverage in our goals for equality. Instead, we pour money into major corporations that are silent during our fight for freedom.

The companies we support need to support us, and we must develop consciousness when we are spending Black dollars. Which side of this fight do these companies align with? Are they allies? Are they on the moral side of history? If we can't answer that—if a company is silent and absent from the fight—then we shouldn't be spending with them. We can no longer allow our dollars to uphold the generational wealth of racist systems. When we unite and pull our collective dollar from a company, that blow is felt. Presently, green is the only common language that the afflicted share with the majority. The Montgomery Bus Boycott shows us that when we stop giving them access to our wealth, they will bend to meet our demands for equality. The question becomes, what discomforts are we willing to endure to be heard?

THE NON-PROTESTER

John Lewis called it good trouble. That's what protesters get themselves into. Trouble. Trouble that's worth the marred public record, the attacks by right-wing media, the bruised wrists from handcuffs, the arrests and sleeping in dirty jail cells. Every day I open my eyes, I get into good trouble for this movement; some days the trouble is more severe than others. I understand that kind of sacrifice, good trouble, is not feasible for everyone. There are people at home who can't actively engage for reasons of health, of family, of distance, of circumstance, but there are other ways to participate in the pursuit of equality without showing up to massive demonstrations. Protests are reactions to injustice. We talked about those catalyst moments that send people into the streets. The police beatings, the unjust shootings, the murders. If you're the person looking at the news with a heavy heart who isn't ready for the action of the streets, there are other ways you can help fuel the cause.

The first way to be supportive is to donate. Give money to organizations that further the pursuit of justice and equality. A person's priorities are tied heavily to what he/she/they is/are willing to invest in. Invest in Black lives. Invest in the bail funds for organizers who are arrested while on the front lines. Donate to inner-city programs. If financial investment isn't possible, invest your time. Get into the communities to become acquainted with the people who live there. Broaden your perspective on cultures unlike your own. Our communities can all be very separated at times, but to get to know a group of people who you have preconceived notions about can help you get rid of stereotypes that were created by this country's jaded eye toward history. The more we blur those lines of separation between communities, the more our humanity will make room for better relations between unique groups of people. You don't have to look like me to love me. You don't have to share my experiences to enjoy learning about them. You don't have to live where I live to empathize with the events that take place there. You don't have to be rich to care. There are many organizations you can donate to, local and national. My organization is Until Freedom, and there are many others who do good work in our communities. Do your research to find an organization both local and national that needs support.

Another way to help is the most obvious of all. Everyone has work to do at home. We all need to be working within our own communities to tease out those ties that bind us all together. To work on shifting the perspectives of our friends, of our family members, of our neighbors.

White people are born with a privilege that gives them power over other communities, especially the Black community. No one living today asked for this privilege. Many may not even realize its presence. It is not easy to see four-dimensionally, past the day-to-day and into the unspoken advantages and disadvantages we get born into. In America, fair skin earns freedom from suspicion and second chances that I and my Black brothers and sisters almost never get. It's on us to use our positions in society to better the position of others. To be the one to reach across the aisle, not to sit quietly while we wait for someone else to take the first step.

Too often we sit among our loved ones, allowing them to get away with racism and bias, and we think outsiders won't see. Assumptions, prejudice, even jokes that seem harmless, all contribute to the idea of a hierarchy where white is better or white is right. Stop allowing stereotypes and dehumanization to happen right in front of you. You cannot be anti-racist and allow racism to happen right in front of you. Use your voice to open the discussion even when there are no minorities at the table. Have our back when no one is looking. What you do when we are not present defines your true standpoint on racism in America. Are you laughing at stereotypical Black jokes? Are you allowing the usage of racial slurs? Are you in support of hoarding resources for your own community but neglecting to be inclusive of others? Are you justifying the discriminatory opinions of people you know? If so, you're just as guilty.

HOLD YOUR PEOPLE ACCOUNTABLE

I know it's uncomfortable to have these hard conversations. A lot of times we are hesitant to approach the topic with people from fear of being exposed for thinking differently than those we love most, but we need to challenge them. Call them out. Let them know that their narrow, racist views about other groups of people are not okay. Even within the Black and brown communities, assumptions are made. Racism and bias exist where they are not checked. They propagate and spread over time when they are not pulled out at the root.

Above all, be active. No matter how you decide to participate, action must always come above inaction. You can't be team non-racist and have no personal involvement in the cause. This goes for those who are a part of the impacted communities, but it's even more essential for allies outside the community. There is a reason you so often see white allies standing in front of Black protesters in the streets. There is a reason why we are so appreciative of white bystanders who pull over and get involved when they see Black men and women interacting with the police. White citizens receive a different standard of treatment when dealing with the law. When allies are able to utilize their privilege as a shield to protect the well-being of Black activists, that is undoubtedly the biggest contribution to the movement one can make. Cops are less ready to escalate physical violence against white activists. They are less ready to deploy pepper spray and tear gas when it is clear their targets will not be only Black and brown. Alliances with white activists equalize the power imbalances seen in the field when we demonstrate for the rights we all deserve.

KARENISM

Here is where I've saved my moment to speak directly to white women. Know from the start that I'm not coming for you. This isn't a conversation that's rooted in aggression. It's about enlightenment. There is a complexity to this discussion that gets lost over Twitter and Instagram and even on TV. It's woman-to-woman talk because all women share common challenges. It's a second level of discrimination and struggle we face together each day. We can relate to being held to different standards than our peers, to having our work questioned and opinions dismissed. However, it's still important to level with the fact that our racial and gender struggles are not the same.

In the past few years, we've seen this background discussion of intersectional unrest turned into a meme online; there's been a lot of talk about "Karens." You might think it's a joke—and it is—but it is a joke that sits on top of a real issue. In the way I understand and experience it, "Karen" is used to signify the disrespect people of color often encounter from white women.

It is because all women have a history of being denied our own rights that white women can better understand the Black community's struggles for equality than white men. White women know what it's like to be fractionated. In the measure of worthiness, using America's scale, white men stand at the top of the hierarchy. They are the good ol' boys. The founders.

They're the ones who put their heads together to establish the laws we follow as a society. They are the highest-valued, most respected citizens in this country. They aren't underpaid. They aren't undereducated. They aren't judged at first sight when they walk in the door of a business. They have passed the generational baton of privilege for hundreds of years. White women come right behind them. To this day, we and our male counterparts aren't paid equally. Women are judged by what we wear, by our decision to have children, by who we marry, by the way we wear our hair, by the color lipstick we choose. Yes, I relate to you on that level. Based on the unequal scale that women are weighed on when compared to men, I'm with you in that fight. But racial inequality is not that same fight. While you understand inequality, you don't understand it from a Black perspective, and failing to see that difference is where even allies to the Black and freedom movements can cause serious harm. There's a level of bias that even the most committed freedom advocate struggles to see.

So let's revisit what "Karen" means. A Karen is a white woman who uses her white privilege as a weapon. There are two types of Karens. There is the Karen who is unapologetic about racist beliefs and who weaponizes skin color, using her whiteness to advance a victim narrative against a Black person. We see this every single day. This is one of the instances of racism that social media has called out and put a spotlight on, but it is not a new innovation. So often in history, the justification for the lynching and murder of Black men in the Jim

Crow era was a white woman claiming to have been assaulted by Black men. I wrote about Emmett Till earlier, how Carolyn Bryant is reported to have waited sixty-two years to admit she had lied[3]—leveraged white womanhood's association with innocence and purity to sic bands of white men against an innocent young Black boy. How, while it was the act of two vile white men that delivered the painful death, it was the lies of Bryant, a white woman, that caused it. She made herself a victim and used her whiteness as a weapon to turn Emmett Till into a villain. And even with the admission of her lie, Bryant's family saw fit to uphold the injustice again, claiming Bryant had been misunderstood.[4] This is the worst type of Karen. This is what Karenism unchecked turns into. So while it's a joke online, we can't let humor, used to temper pain, get in the way of the truth underneath it all.

Privilege can't be helped. White people are born with it. It's ingrained in the very fabric of our country. It's rooted in the soil of America. Racism, however, is a choice. When you choose to activate your privilege to bring harm to another community, you're exercising racism. That harm can be physical, emotional, financial, or institutional. Being nonracist means thinking of how your privilege hinders other communities and actively working against that hindrance. A privileged person who chooses to be inactive is complicit in the violence of racism. That may be blunt, that may offend, but it's a fact. Look inside yourself and ask if you're okay with participating in all that means.

The second variety of Karenism involves white women who are much less aware of the ways in which they may weaponize their whiteness. These are the "All Lives Matter" people. The message is technically true. The Black community would love to be able to focus on all lives. Our mission is to reach a point where history can mark the date when all lives begin to matter equally, but that is not our reality today. Unfortunately, that has never been our reality. A Black person in America wakes in the morning and goes to sleep at night being told that we do not matter. The message is reiterated every day on our TV screens. The message is reinforced with every denied loan application, with every job passed down by nepotism over merit, and with every unequal dollar poured into inner-city school systems. Black lives don't matter, and until they do, screaming that all lives matter is racist. This second type of Karen is much more passive in their approach to Black people. They often intend to do well and come with the intent to help. They provide support but only if the movement takes shape in a way that's familiar to them. When movement leadership conflicts with their notions of what's right, this type of Karen retreats to emotional manipulation. When in conflict with a brown or Black person of color, the passive-aggressive Karen uses tears and even lies to gain emotional leverage. While not overtly racist, this approach reinforces stereotypes that Black people are aggressive.

This was my experience while planning the Women's March on Washington. I struggle when talking about the Women's March. I feel like I need more pages than this book allows to express how I, as the only Black chairperson of that movement, was targeted and attacked. The day to tell that full story is coming. It was difficult to organize with many white women who had never been a part of a social justice movement before. There were all these new faces and freshman voices attempting to come together on behalf of women's rights with no true racial justice lens. In particular, I got concerned early on when I saw a lack of awareness around the racial issues that sit alongside the women's rights issues we targeted. I recall a particular moment of despair when Bob Bland, a white woman and one of the other chairpersons, looked me in the eyes and asked what race had to do with women's rights. I was horrified because I knew her lack of understanding was not unique among the organizers. We had a lot of intense discussions and were publicly attacked. After all we endured, Bob now understands our plight. It makes me proud to watch her articulate the cause in front of her peers.

White women rushed to the movement, and while I knew the power of the moment, I was also aware that because some in leadership alongside me weren't as experienced in activism, their potential to be dangerous was high. They had no REAL understanding or commitment to Black life. They thought they could relate, but their connection to our struggle was not rooted in substance. If you haven't dealt with racism that's close to you, you can't adequately address the racism of the world. You don't know what it feels like. You don't know the repercussions of it. You can't even always identify it, at times when it's staring you in your face. Every time I suggested that we integrate the disparity between Black, brown, and immigrant women in comparison to white women, the direction of the march became uncomfortable for too many. They didn't realize that their experience as white women was not the same as the experience of women of color. We couldn't march for their right to choose and ignore the specific nuances of Black and women of color as it relates to reproductive health. The issue wasn't that they were against bringing up race. They just didn't want to upset other people, so they tried to avoid the most important topics.

We rejected this, and when we demanded that the Women's March be inclusive of our issues pertaining to womanhood and race, I got labeled as the angry Black woman in the room, accused of being divisive. Women of color contend with the issues of reproductive health, lower wages, and prejudice against us in our childbearing years. Those prejudices are universal. White women and women of color relate on those issues, but there is a subset of challenges that apply after the universal needs for women have been met. For instance, Black women are paid less than white women in corporate America. Black and brown women receive lower-quality gynecological care; they often have no access to health insurance or even a regular doctor to rely on. White women wanted to protest, but they didn't want to put all our issues on the table. They came to the table but weren't prepared to sit through every course of the meal, and when something served wasn't to their taste, they became uncomfortable. In the face of a Black woman demanding representation of issues that plague women who look like me, I became the villain of that movement. The "Karens" helping to organize this massive movement were perpetuating the very inequality we were supposed to be protesting. Of course, this is not about every individual white woman who helped organize the march. My truth relates to how people operate as a group.

It was one of the most trying times of my life, one that I still haven't recovered from professionally, emotionally, and politically. It is a time that I prefer to let other women speak on, because when I've spoken, my words have often been misconstrued and used against me. I hand these pages over to my sister and accomplice Linda Sarsour, a woman who walks shoulder to shoulder in the movement for Black lives. She is a feminist. A Palestinian-American activist and fellow co-chair of the Women's March. She is a woman who understands that equality is a privilege that should be universal. She could hoard her efforts for the Palestinian community, she could pick and choose when and how to activate for her community because the Palestinian people face their own struggle, but she doesn't. She stands up for her community and all other communities humanity has done a disservice. She is my sister, my accomplice, and someone I look up to in this space because she has committed to righteousness regardless of race, skin tone, or religion. Linda Sarsour chases freedom aggressively, without apology, and without bias. I will share her perspective because my version of my mistreatment may sound biased; it may be discounted as angry or exaggerated because Black women aren't allowed to feel. Remember the rules I taught you? I'm following them even in my own book because for the majority of people reading, the white women and men taking in this narrative, my word will not be enough. In fact, I'm adding another rule: Black people must always have a witness to prove their truth. So, I pass the mic for a few pages . . .

WOMEN'S MARCH THROUGH THE EYES OF
CO-CHAIR LINDA SARSOUR

Before people started coining the term "Karens," we came face-to-face with them at the 2017 Women's March. That movement became the largest single-day demonstration in American history, but it took a significant amount of effort to ensure that it was representative of all women. Tamika, Carmen Perez, and I were in the minority, representing women of color and marginalized women. We found ourselves not only having to organize but having to teach the white women involved about how to organize with us. We weren't looking for allies in that movement. We needed accomplices. Allies show up to the movement but don't have to sacrifice anything to be present. Accomplices make an intentional decision to show up for the movement knowing sacrifice is inevitable. They commit knowing that their jobs may be at stake or perhaps family members may be in opposition to the cause. There is something they could potentially lose. Despite these sacrifices, they still show up because they are committed to freedom and equality. Many white women involved in the Women's March did not want to give up the cushion that exists in their normal lives. They turned their activism on and off, flipping the switch when they went back home to their husband or their job. They didn't want the stain of the movement to bleed onto the fabric of their privilege. They didn't want to venture into uncomfortable terrain, but that is what is needed.

We are in a state of emergency. We do not need people who show up when they feel comfortable. We need commitment. Most white women only want to talk about stereotypical issues, and yes, those are important, but when we began to talk about equal pay within racial groups of women and we looked at the disparity in privileges white women receive over all other women, they started squirming. They didn't want to talk about that. They didn't want to protest their own privilege. We had eight hundred thousand followers on our social media platforms, and we began to look at the discrepancy of equal pay, pointing out that white women make more than Black women, than Latinx women, than immigrant women. The divisive accusations began there. Even a *New York Times* reporter wrote a story about us, calling us divisive, when we were simply trying to give white women a perspective of women of color that they had not considered before. They didn't want to complicate the march. Focus on Trump is what they told us. Controversy was swirling because we wanted to interject race into the conversation. White women avoid courageous conversation about race. They walk away from it. Tamika isn't a leader who allows the conversation to be avoided. We agreed to help co-chair the movement, but with our participation came that discomfort. We represent communities where race is the most dominant challenge that hinders opportunity and equity in American society. We cannot and will not allow our faces to become tokens in a movement to prove that it is diverse, if diverse issues aren't on the agenda. White women want one issue at a time. As Audre Lorde taught us, we cannot have single-issue struggles because we do not live single-issue lives.

We gave our presence and our platforms to the Women's March because we knew that it could happen without us. White women would organize a march, and the media would say it represented us all. We had to ensure that Black women's issues were addressed. Muslim-American women were represented. Latinx-Americans were heard. We had women from Flint, Michigan, representing the water crisis. We had trans women present, sharing their struggles. None of these diverse communities would have been centered had it not been for us demanding a microphone for the problems pertaining to the rights of women of color. What they called divisive, we called inclusive, and that inclusion never would have happened had Tamika, Carmen Perez, and I not been involved. Tamika bore the brunt of the frustration. White women are not accustomed to being held accountable by a Black woman, but everything Tamika did during that movement was normal. She brought up circumstances of inequality for women outside the majority. She was attacked because she wouldn't go along with ready-made plans.

We saw this in the 2020 vice presidential debates. The world watched Kamala Harris under a microscope. She sat through ninety minutes of gaslighting and disrespect, forced to smile, to go along, to not appear angry. She had to keep complete composure and display no emotion lest she be labeled an angry Black woman. She had to figure out how to navigate through the disrespect without falling into the trap of a stereotype. That is the reality for Black women. It was the reality for Tamika, and she was railroaded when the media picked up the false narrative accusing her of being divisive and angry. It goes back to the notion of all it takes is the word of a white woman to criminalize people of color. Tamika was made into the villain for requesting a microphone for outlying communities when her only intention was to be inclusive of the issues women from communities of color struggle with. White women in that movement had to be held accountable for the promises they were making. If we're going to march for women, we must march for ALL women.

We refused to let our communities' voices be drowned out. We had to look at the nooks and crannies of every community. We were accused of coming to the table to consolidate power, and I saw nothing wrong with that. Of course we wanted to gain power for our people. We would not allow ourselves to be tokens on a white stage. We wanted equity from the march. Black women should fight for Black women. I wanted to make sure my people had a seat at the table because Muslim-American women have a different set of needs than other communities. Tamika also wanted to organize a women's leadership conference in Detroit. It was called Reclaiming Our Time. It felt insane to turn around and plan another event so quickly. The division from the Women's March had us on one side and the white women on another, but I know Tamika well enough to know that when we put the right people in place, we can accomplish anything. So we did it. We did it scared. We did it tired. We did it worn out, and most of all, we did it without major support. Many of the white women who had just marched side by side with us were no longer willing to help, but we didn't need them. Tamika was never worried. She told me that we didn't need them because we had our ancestors, and sure enough, those ancestors carried us through. There were eight people on our planning committee, mostly people of color, and we mobilized more than five thousand attendees at Cobo Hall in Detroit. People spend two years planning an event of that size, and we did it in two and a half months. Without substantial help. This lifestyle takes faith because circumstances feel impossible.

The odds are always stacked against advocates for freedom. You have to believe change will come despite the pitfalls; despite the traps of democracy, you have to keep going. This fight wears you down. It takes every bit of you. I've seen Tamika's stress and perseverance wear her down to ninety-nine pounds because she was carrying the pursuit of freedom on her back. It's heavy, but I am committed to carrying the weight with her. I ignore the ailments. The ulcers, the hospital stays, the weight loss. I keep marching forward even when it hurts because I believe in Tamika, I believe in myself, and I trust the integrity of our mission. We will not stop. She does not give up or give in, although people have tried to silence her. They have tried to force their narrative on her, tried to turn her into someone she is not. Tamika challenged white women to use their privilege to stand up for marginalized women. She stood in front of thousands of people and called white women to action, and the ones who were genuine in their commitment responded. They listened. It was inevitable that a Black woman able to move the needle in the way that Tamika can would become a target of the patriarchy. She became too powerful, too influential, and not just within marginalized communities. She began to influence the wives of white men in power.

I had an inkling that after these women began to support Tamika, we were in trouble. It was then that people began to dig for something in Tamika's past to invalidate her. Detractors of this movement combed through four hours of video at Minister Farrakhan's Saviours' Day just to spot her in the crowd. That was all they could find to use against her. Her attendance at a community event. There was nothing to expose about her, so they went grasping for straws. She was becoming a powerful leader in America, and the patriarchy felt threatened, so they began to dig up dirt. I wasn't shocked by the defamation of her character. Her personal respect for Minister Farrakhan wasn't the issue. That was merely the scapegoat. The true issue was Tamika, every time she spoke, giving white women an instruction manual on how to support disenfranchised communities. The smear campaign emerged because white men did not want their wives to follow a Black woman toward equality. Death threats, hate mail, intimidation tactics poured in, but none of it worked.

Those of us who are in allyship with Tamika remain there. Are we scared? At times, yes, but guess what? We do it scared. A state of emergency requires a state of courage that demands your involvement even if you are unsure that you will live to see the mission to the end. You must be willing to commit your life for freedom, and in order to make that commitment, leadership must be strong. Tamika is that leader. She doesn't ask you to do something that she hasn't done herself. If she expects you to stand up to militarized police forces, she's right there with you, toe to toe, in the face of shields and guns, being pepper-sprayed, being arrested. If she asks you to vote, she's going state to state rallying voters, making sure people are registered and mailing in her absentee ballot at the same time. If she's asking you to use your voice and protest injustice, she's doing the same, with a microphone in front of her, with the scope of the opposition targeting her. She uses her platform, and she tells an authentic truth, a story of pain, of frustration. She says all the things a publicist would tell you not to say. She is the voice of the people, so it doesn't have to be politically correct. Her pain and the pain of her community are what she expresses. There is no censoring of her message because she is a self-made leader to this movement.

One thing about Tamika is she can't be bought. When we agreed to bring women of color to the Women's March, we had one condition: We refused to work with corporate sponsors. I raised money from prominent nonprofits, and we called all our personal friends for donations because we didn't want to sell our voice. We didn't want to stand in front of a Walmart sign and be conscious of saying things that were agreeable to corporations. When you aren't for sale, your voice can't be controlled to reflect a corporate narrative. You can't speak on controversial issues when your funding comes from the institution. Tamika is free. Everything that has given her notoriety in this fight is because she has done and said things that others are afraid to speak on. She calls things as they are and is willing to take the consequences that come along with that. She's willing to be uncomfortable for freedom. Tamika stands in her power and is proof to a new generation of activists that you can be powerful and influential by being your unapologetic self. She is exactly who she says she is and must be protected at all costs.

BUILDING IT UP TOGETHER

The Women's March and the years that followed taught me perseverance. There were many storms afterward. There were many spotlights shone on me, targeting me, the Black woman, the angry woman. The media put me on a stage to execute me. It felt like a symbolic lynching of my character to discredit the trust I had earned both within and outside my community. It was a public attack, but despite the emotional toll it took, I endured. I received the lessons that came with leadership. I realized that everyone who shows up as a friend to the mission is not committed to the same level of activism that I am. I live in the movement. I can't escape it. I can't turn it off. I cannot put it down and come back to it later. It is a twenty-four-hour-per-day commitment. I live in the house assigned to freedom fighting, so whatever goes wrong within it, I must figure out how to fix. You don't abandon the entire house just because a window breaks or a furnace kicks the bucket. You repair it. You build it up so that it's stronger and can accommodate as the family grows, and although I welcome guests, guests must realize they are only visiting. If you are a guest to a movement, respect house rules. It is the responsibility of the offended community to decide the rules of engagement for the movement.

It's important for allies from the white community to be involved. We welcome everyone to join us in this fight for equality. We're fighting for Black lives, but we aren't excluding any voice from contributing to that cause. But our allies need to be conscious of the fact that they get to press pause on this fight. They get to raise hell with us, to be loud with us, to link arms with us and fight side by side, but at the end of the day, they still have the option to go home. They get to separate themselves from the burden of the fight and go back to their lives, where they are still a part of the privileged majority. They get to put the burden down when it gets heavy. It isn't theirs to hold on to.

We cannot set our burdens down. The struggle continues after we disengage. The struggle is like a cape to our allies. They can put it on and take it off when they want, but we are the struggle personified. Our skin isn't detachable. We engage in the movement every time we leave our homes. Our fight is lifelong. We breathe it every second of every day.

When allies activate with us, they must be careful not to try to own the fight. It's easy to get sucked up into the spotlight of it all. The news makes what I do look heroic when, really, it's just who I am. It's all I know. I'm not making a choice to stand up for justice; this walk of life chose me. I would be on this journey whether I had a million cameras on me or none. So I don't need to "own" the moment. I don't need to be the voice of this movement, but when the movement is co-opted by those determined to change or soften its message, I see it as another form of privilege and racism—but even more insidious, because those attacks now come from inside the house. Allies who activate must do so with consideration and respect that this is not their experience. The consequences to these protests will not affect their communities.

White allies, let me be clear, we welcome you. We want you with us, but what we do not need are more drivers trying to navigate the direction of the movement. Don't make the fight about you. Do it selflessly. Be a part of it because it's the right thing to do, not as a self-serving way to gain control and attention. The spotlight should ALWAYS be on the issues of injustice and inequality, never on an individual white person.

Those entering from the outside must remember that a painful and hard-fought path led us to this current struggle. When we think of Black oppression, we tend to think it was a long time ago. Black people were enslaved for longer than we've been free. For some of us, being enslaved is all the history we know. Without the help of professional sources, we can't trace our lineage back to the villages our ancestors come from in Africa. We have been disenfranchised from that truth. Our native languages were stripped. Our native customs, erased. Who we are and where we come from as Black "Americans" began with bondage.

Even after emancipation, Black people in this country have been subjected to suppressive and oppressive periods of time that hinder the community from attaining true equity in an American society. Freedom is relative. Even after emancipation, the sentiment of enslavement still thickened the air. Laws replaced chains enforcing a system that left underserved communities out of opportunities to build wealth and shape the social systems that guide our lives in America. Black children forced to run home to beat the streetlights, in hopes of avoiding backroad dangers in a sundown town, were not free. Black men murdered simply because of an accusation and without trial are not free. Black people who cannot drink from the same water fountain or use the same restrooms as whites are not free. Black people who eat Skittles and wear a hoodie are not free. Black people who can't listen to music at a loud volume without being murdered are not free. America gave us the illusion of freedom, but oppression itself is a form of bondage. We've been segregated, we've been redlined, we've been drugged, we've been robbed of the right to vote. Our post-slavery era has been a product of the mental conditioning that was done during enslavement. America remains racist. There is no way to sugarcoat that.

We've fought to escape that broken identity ever since, but the damage is not fixable overnight. This is the work. People of color have fought for every right we have. Nothing was given. Nothing was easy. From the right to be educated, to the right to vote, it was all fought for. Those things are wins against a long system of inequality, a system put in place to stifle Black people and exterminate our race. This is the same fight. A racist system that took 246 years to build takes just as long to be amended. So, allies, when you join us in this fight, realize that the country you love, the flag you hail, the system that represents the land of the free and the home of the brave, it represents something different for the Black community. Lend your voice, lend your presence, but be teachable and be empathetic to what our communities have endured as you call yourself a friend to the movement.

Twelve
Equal Justice Under the Law

ACCOUNTABLE TO, BY, AND FOR US

Accountability is big for me. Politicians on the right will tell you they're for accountability too, but that word can be interpreted in many ways. The "law and order" mentality that gets talked about on campaign trails never gets applied equally. Most people in the Black community want people held accountable when their actions lead to the murder of innocent Black citizens. Some believe we should completely dismantle and abolish prisons and police and create entirely new models of public safety. I talked about this earlier, and yes, we need an overhaul. But until that point in time, it is imperative that we drain the racism from the criminal justice system we have. There is a scale of justice in America, and Black citizens have always been punished at the highest level. That extends from petty crime and drug possession cases turning into lifelong burdens up through the worst of the worst. We just spent years literally watching (via social media) cops go unpunished for killing innocent Black people all across this country. We watched a teenager drive into town with an AR-15, hoping for a gunfight with advocates for Black lives, getting it, killing two men in cold blood, and walking away scot-free.

We need to tear down and reimagine models of public safety because the criminal legal system was built to surveil, punish, and control Black, brown, and marginalized communities, which is why the system treats white people so differently. But there are some steps we can take in the meantime as harm reduction. One first step is to address rampant racial disparities. That's what we were promised, and it's what we must get. Any harm motivated by racism is a hate crime and should be treated as such. Holding white folks to the letter of the law without tipping the scale to lessen the consequence is mandatory on our path to ending racism. We have to stop making excuses for injustice. We must begin recognizing these crimes for what they are. Any injury done to a person of color that is motivated by resentment and hatred of one's skin color is an act of domestic terrorism. I'm calling it out. Stop excusing hate. When a white man waves a gun around looking to scare off protesters, that's a terroristic act. When he bombs a downtown Nashville city block, that's domestic terrorism. The bigger crime is that the media doesn't even acknowledge white terrorism. There is a sense of entitlement in the doctrine of white supremacy that makes supremacists believe they are above the law. Whenever a slap on the wrist is given as punishment for a crime committed against a person of color, it is a message to other racists that says the criminal legal system supports discrimination. That's why we need to radically transform public safety, because these systems will never be our savior. But until we build the world where Black people can live free of police and vigilante violence, we need swift and punitive action against cops and any other person who applies racism that harms people of color. There should be automatic charges for cops who kill people when there should have been another outcome. There must be immediate firing of officers who discharge their weapon when another nonlethal course of action is an option. There are too many situations where unarmed Black people end up dead when encountering cops and vigilantes.

Too often the Black victims of these crimes are vilified to justify the actions of their murderers. The media immediately begins an assassination of the victim's character and excuses police officers who band together like gang members. We saw this with George Floyd's death. There were other officers on the scene, protecting Derek Chauvin as he shoved his knee into George Floyd's neck. Not one of them intervened. Not one of them went against what they knew was wrong to stop the murder of an innocent and unarmed man. The only thug on the streets that day was the officer who was hiding racist intentions behind his badge. Chauvin was the rare police officer convicted of violating Black lives, but make no mistake--one bad apple doesn't save the bunch. Over 200 Black Americans were killed by police in 2021, the year of his conviction. 27% of the dead from 13% of the population.

We must stop giving domestic terrorists the authority to take lives. Police officers have a monumental responsibility to keep people safe, but that has never meant Black people or people of color. When systems are motivated by racism and hate, they become the threat. Who will protect my Black son from the threat of the police? There were no innocent cops at the scene of George Floyd's murder. Doing nothing was a crime that day. Officers of the law take an oath to serve and protect, but too many (meaning ANY) filter that protection; they serve with bias. Black people are being hunted.

THE OVERSEERS OF HISTORY

This is what white men used to do in the South when slaves worked the fields. They sat on their horse with their rifle over their shoulder and their revolver in a holster. Lurking. Waiting. Harassing. Mistreating. Enforcing. When they decided to pull a trigger on a slave in the field, no one blinked, and no punishment was given. We aren't too far from that legacy of enslavement. It feels the same. A white man murders a Black person, and the institution begins its search for reasons of acceptability. Reparation for the loss of life cannot be debatable. A change must come, and we must revoke that legacy of power given to overseers.

We've paid tribute to the brutal legacy of bondage for too long. The unspoken hierarchy, the memorializing of murderers who history has written in as heroes. Declaring national holidays for men like Christopher Columbus, erecting monuments for Confederate generals like Robert E. Lee, naming highways after John C. Calhoun in South Carolina, flying Confederate flags over state buildings in the South. All of it helps to establish an unspoken oppression over Black people in this country. It's a slap in the face and a narcissistic ode to the brutal history of one of the most inhumane acts on this earth. That moment in history has leaked onto every generation since. It is a stain. It is a disgrace. But it is a sentiment that the institution keeps alive by celebrating these figures. They are not heroes. They were domestic terrorists, and the legion of white supremacists who carry on that hatred are domestic terrorists. We have to stop celebrating a history that haunts people of color. The mental conditioning is traumatizing. Hitler and Mussolini are not held up as heroes to be studied and admired. They are embarrassments. They are stains on the history of their homelands. Their governments worked to wash those people and their messages of hate and bloodlust out of society's fabric. So why do *we* celebrate inhumanity, acts of murder, rape, kidnapping, torture of citizens of this country? You must all see, white, brown, indigenous, Latinx, and Asian, how living in a country that celebrates our ancestral pain is damaging to the Black community. Value us. Make amends to us, with overdue reparations and with our damn respect. It's the least that can be done. Stop protecting murderers. Stop celebrating our executioners. I am tasking America with the duty of holding the murderers of people of color accountable.

RECLAIMING BLACK TRUST AND INTIMACY

Accountability doesn't end with one community, however. It's not just about feeling safe within the institution. An issue for Black America is feeling safe among our own. The Black community already has the weight of racism on its back. That burden is heavy. It becomes backbreaking when we don't carry it together. There is a struggle for power within the Black community between men and women. It is not by chance. It has nothing to do with the Black woman's attitude or the Black man's desire to abandon his family. It's by design, and it stems from enslavement. Black women feel unprotected by the Black man. Black men feel disrespected by the Black woman. I feel this tension within our community every day. It is old roots from a rotting tree that "massa" planted. Rape was common during the era of enslavement, and many children were the product of it. During these violent interactions, Black men were held at bay, forced to stand by, and unable to protect Black women. They couldn't intervene when slave masters forced themselves into the beds of their sisters, wives, daughters. The feeling of resentment mounted on both sides. Black women feeling abandoned by Black men, and Black men forced to feel inadequate for doing nothing. It was a physical assault against women but a mental assault against Black men. That void is still there. It is a dark tradition passed down from generation to generation.

As a Black woman in the movement, I look around and I see my sisters out there with me. If a Black man is killed unjustly, we are out there, fists in the air, lending our lives, our voices, our time to a movement that demands the safety of our Black brothers. It makes me sad that I don't see as many Black men showing up for Black women in that same way. I have my close-knit brothers who show up for me all the time. I'm protected by them, of course, but as a community, we as Black women lack that protection. We see it in the streets of protest, we see it in political engagement. Black men will not like this part, but we got to talk about it, because if I'm telling you, Black woman to Black man, that I feel unprotected, I feel a void in your commitment to show up for me—for us—if I'm telling you that too many Black women feel this way, you must listen.

Ask yourself: Why aren't you showing up to the movement when we are disrespected? Why aren't you intervening when we are in danger? Why aren't you present? And on the flip side, I'll ask myself some things. I'll bring the conversation to my sisters. Black women. Why do we question the worthiness of a Black man's place in our community, in our home, in our bed? We have to be accountable to one another. How can we demand that other communities begin to have the conversation about where their hatred for Black people came from if we can't converse among ourselves to figure our own mess out?

We must face our history, dialogue about our mistrust in one another, and learn to listen to one another. Only when the two principal forces of the Black community—the Black woman and the Black man—function as a unit can we win a war from the outside. We can't gain traction in this fight because we don't stand together enough. I have had Black men challenge my leadership. I watched Black men align themselves with Trump's politics because they thought his financial plans benefited them. We can't focus on single-issue politics. If the financial strength of the Black man is more important than the reproductive rights of Black women, and Black men are willing to vote for the opposition just to line their pockets, we have a problem. We have a loyalty issue. Protecting Black women, Black children, Black communities, must precede all else. We are not powerful when we are aligned on different sides of the fence, and I challenge every Black man and woman reading this book to take on the task of beginning the conversation. Let's drop the defense mechanisms so we can relate to one another. Black men hold other Black men accountable, and Black women need to do the same. Only after we have figured out our own relationships inside the community will our relationships with others change, because then we will be facing other communities hand in hand, not as adversaries.

This idea that the Black woman doesn't need the Black man. It's not true. We have had to accommodate your absence because the system has locked you up, has demonized you, has killed you, so yes, the Black woman adapted. We've functioned in survival mode without you. Black women adapted to the environment of raising children alone, but we need you. You belong at the table of leadership, of activism, because our strategy to gain equality does not work without you. Black lives—Black men's lives—matter!

Thirteen

Cannot Stand

ROOTING FOR EVERYONE BLACK

I've been writing a lot about the white majority, the patriarchal ancestors whose privilege has been inherited from the colonial establishment. But now I'm going to talk about the rest of America. The seasoning to the melting pot that makes up these great states. The Latinx flavor, the Asian flavor, the African flavor, the Middle Eastern flavor, the Native American flavor: all the different races of people that make America so diverse. There is a line of demarcation that exists between each community in relation to the Black community. In hierarchical ranking, African American people are at the bottom of the totem pole. A narrative has been told that the Black community has no value. They call us dangerous, they call us lazy, they call us uneducated, they paint pictures of our children as uncivilized, our women are accused of manipulating the system. The defamation of the community has made Black people pariah in chief. Even other minority groups in America have disassociated their lineage with us. Melanin or lack thereof has been used to divide the Latinx community for centuries. Groups within the Latinx community are seduced by perceived proximity to whiteness, encouraged to negate their African ancestry. Skin color and hair texture are used as a justification to dispel African roots and to create distance between Latin Americans and African Americans, but the diaspora is real. The transatlantic slave trade is a historic tragedy that cannot be erased. More than ten million African slaves were sold in South America and the Caribbean. Yes, you read that right. Only a small fraction of Africans were sold in North America, about four hundred thousand slaves, to be more accurate.[1] That's only 4.4 percent of slaves abducted from Africa. Many of the rest were sold in the Caribbean and South America. So don't tell me this fight doesn't apply to the Latinx community. Latinx Americans are of African ancestry. It doesn't matter how light your skin is, we are connected. The plight of the Black community is your fight too, but there is a tension that exists between us. I challenge the broader Latinx communities all the time to come forward and add their voice to the march toward equality. There are leaders like Rosa Clemente, an Afro Latina, and Carmen Perez, a Mexican American, who work hard to be representatives at the table when racial issues arise, but there is an overwhelming lack of Latinx engagement in freedom movements. Carmen and I were two of the four co-chairs of the Women's March, but we have been in the streets fighting for equality for years. She is a shining example of going above and beyond for people of color. Where I considered her an ally, she taught me that being an ally was not enough. She wanted to be in this freedom fight with me as an accomplice and she is my sister. She is a great example in the Latinx community of what it means to stand with the Black community. We need our sisters and brothers in the Latinx community to stand with us and to challenge the patriarchal system to change.

The African community is also underrepresented and disconnected when Black people deal with injustice. They see our plight as a suffering outside of their existence. It is one of the challenges of being Black in America. My usage of "Black America" in contrast to "African American" is intentional. Ancestry links Black Americans to Africa, but the majority of us are without true connection to the motherland. Enslavement robbed us of our religion, our customs, our native languages, our native remedies. We were left with a blank canvas that was colored in over time by our oppressors. The ancestors who were well versed in African customs were spread throughout the country, villages split, families fractured. Not all slaves came from the same place in Africa. There was a language barrier. There is a myth that Africa is this monolithic place. It is an entire continent filled with different cultures, religions, practices, and tongues. Slaves who were abducted didn't all share the same ethnicity. They were from different tribes, which created ethnolinguistic barriers. These different tribes were forced together to make the journey across the Atlantic. The only thing they had in common was their continent of origin. They couldn't even communicate their fears with one another. Once they made it to their respective plantations, they were forbidden to speak in their native languages. English was forced on slaves to prevent the possibility of unheard plots to rebel. Christianity was forced, and African religions and customs were stripped. Enslaved Africans became property of the plantation. Ancestors who died in that first generation took with them any attachment to Africa. So, I relate to Blackness in America because all things that would have made me know the African parts of myself were stolen from me.

We have the blood of Africa without having the knowledge and emotional connection to the continent. Many Black Americans need ancestry tracing to even identify which tribe they come from. It is because of this stripping during enslavement that there is a disconnect from our African brethren. Most don't know us. Most don't claim us. There is a sentiment that African Americans are not "original" enough to truly be "African." There is an elitist view that sees African Americans as a subset class. It's a sentiment that our lineage to Africa is diluted. Wherever slave ships touched is where we will occupy, but our DNA, our omega, is Africa. Our skin is Black, and while our customs and history may differ, this American institution views us the same. There is no line of demarcation that cops see when we find ourselves under the target of their gun. This struggle is your struggle too. You are a part of this global issue of inequality alongside us, despite our differences. It is a collective conversation and a common problem. Disunity will not keep you safe, it will not stall the trigger of a racist cop or infuse your children's schools with equal funding. The false promises of being "nearer" to whiteness is as false for native Africans as it is for every other ethnic minority in this country. You are affected by what ails the Black community, whether you want to be or not, so it serves us best to stand in solidarity.

Other minority groups in America may not have direct lineage to Black folks, but we all have a moral obligation to protect humanity. What we have seen in recent history defies morality. The killing of our men, women, and children is inhumane. I take no pride in the suspicion that an 8:46 video of police officers asphyxiating a dog with a bent knee in full uniform would have received a clearer response, less muddled by fear and politics, than the one of our brother George Floyd. If you subscribe to the idea that you are in some group that is placed higher in the hierarchy of privilege in America and you accept the crimes done against Black people, you are contributing to the institution of racism. I challenge all groups of color to ask yourself: Do you show up for marginalized communities? History has shown us that at any moment, any person of color can be targeted. If we are divided, we lack influence. Activism is a numbers game. The more people in protest of inequality, the more accountable the democracy must become. People of color in America must realize that there is no prize for being almost white. The demand to respect, protect, and adequately service marginalized communities who help drive America's economy cannot be optional. Neither can your willingness to stand up for righteousness.

Fourteen
Vote and Build

NOT EITHER/OR BUT BOTH/AND

When I was a child, one of the first analogies that I learned was "You have to be able to walk and chew gum at the same time." At that young age, I thought it was literal, but the true meaning is mastering the ability to multitask. We must be multidimensional as it pertains to our political strategies. When we talk about the voting process and what needs to happen on behalf of our communities, we have to walk and chew gum. We understand that American politics have not been the saving grace for Black people, but that doesn't mean we can abandon politics completely. We have to be able to work toward fixing the issues that harm us while participating in the space. What we need to focus on is building our own economic engines, schools, institutions, and places that are for us, by us, and about us.

US = BLACK PEOPLE

There are many scholars and experts in the financial, educational, and health care fields who have brilliant and extensive plans to do this. You can't not participate in the political process because you don't believe or trust in it. Doing so disregards the millions of Black people who rely on the system to survive. Your family members who rely on government assistance for housing, for health care, for food, for education. You may not participate in it, but I guarantee you, someone you love relies on it. Those things are controlled by everyday politics, and we need every vote to help influence those systems.

I realize that the protest movement is clearly more action-packed in the moments on the ground, but voting is a form of activism. Your vote is a powerful tool that leads this fight for equity and equality. Some days doing the research it takes to make an informed political decision is the protest.

Stopping people of color from voting was a design of a racist past. In today's politics, our oppressors don't have to try very hard. Too many of us are willingly declining to participate, but what I challenge you to consider is why history has tried to suppress the Black vote in the first place.

When someone works that hard to stop you from voting, you have to wonder what kind of power we're losing. Black and brown people must stop deleting themselves from this political power and realize there is a reason why they do not want us to participate. The anti-Black establishment isn't concerned with us eating ourselves to death. They aren't concerned with Black folks drinking ourselves to death. They aren't concerned with us partaking in destructive behaviors like the use of crack cocaine, even though they labeled the use of opioids in suburbia a national crisis. The institution does not actively seek to stop any behavior we engage in that contributes to the destruction of the disenfranchised, but they actively attempt to suppress the votes of people of color. They work hard for or against something only when it benefits them. The "they" I speak of is the operators of the system. They attempt to keep communities of color from the polls because suffrage is where our power lies.

Our ancestors fought for the right to cast a ballot, and it saddens me that so many Black and brown communities neglect to live up to that obligation. As I think back on Election Day 2020, it occurs to me how many people—people I march with, people I fight for, people I know to be committed to the fight for Black lives—don't feel compelled to use their one vote. After watching an election that should not have been close at all run neck and neck, I realize there's a lack of clarity around what those votes really mean. Let me be clear: IF YOU PROTEST BUT DON'T GO TO THE POLLS, YOU HAVEN'T FINISHED THE JOB. Our model should be *protest, politics, policy*. Congressman John Lewis, Medgar Evers, and Dr. King were no fools when they risked their lives for our access to the ballot box. Your vote is your voice. It is one of the most powerful dogs you have in this fight, and if you choose not to unleash your power, you have no room to complain.[1]

ORGANIZE THE POWER

So many people were moved to do something in the wake of the murders of George Floyd and Breonna Taylor. Protesters activated in droves, feeling like enough is enough, but we surpassed the threshold of injustice a long time ago. We have felt the pain of inequality for centuries. We cannot endure anymore. Human life should not have to be taken for people to notice and speak up about the way Black communities are targets for racism. When it gets to the point where police officers are using Black people for target practice, we are already late to the fight. The resistance against racial inequity doesn't start after a trigger has been pulled. It starts with our everyday decisions. It starts at the polls. It starts at the school board meetings, at the city council meetings, it starts in conversations with your friends, with the way you raise your children, it starts with who you select on the ballot.

In 1965 Dr. Martin Luther King, Jr., marched on Selma to bring national attention to the issues faced by citizens in the Jim Crow South when they attempted to involve themselves in politics. The march was inspired by the murder of Jimmie Lee Jackson, a Black man who was beaten and shot by the police for participating in a peaceful voting rights march. His death was one of many along the road toward suffrage rights. Too often we are sparked to protest after someone has been murdered. We seek justice for the death and ignore the everyday occurrences that lead to it. Dr. King said it best:

We must be concerned about not merely who murdered him, but about the system, the way of life, the philosophy that produced the murderer.[2]

We must prosecute the shooters, yes, but we must topple the system that empowers the militarized police force in the first place. Voting helps accomplish that. People were beaten, brutalized, terrorized, and murdered for this generation of Black voters to have the right to peacefully engage in politics.

As I sat in front of the television, phone in one hand, iPad close to the other, checking three different sources for updates on the 2020 presidential election, I saw an election where every vote mattered. Black people in Georgia turned a traditionally red state to blue by voting for Joe Biden and Kamala Harris. The margin for the popular vote was under 0.5 percent of the vote in that state.

One half of one percent!

There are millions of Black and brown voters in this country who didn't make it a priority to make it to the polls. Some didn't have time, others didn't think their singular ballot would make a difference, others were afraid of conflict in a tense political and racial climate. None of those is a good excuse, because there is no excuse. People of color, especially Black people, must learn to move within the system even when you feel like it is rigged against you because even a rigged system will do what it is designed to do. Cause mass destruction if it goes unchecked. You cannot give up when they cheat. Freedom fighters cannot give up when they lie, when they manipulate. We must learn to influence the numbers in concentrated ways that unify our vote to support candidates who bring us closer to our goals. Stacey Abrams, the Black gubernatorial candidate in Georgia's 2018 race, lost the state election for governor in 2018, but she refused to concede the race. She went on record challenging a system that refused voters their rights. The numbers were debatable, and the margin for her loss was a mere 1.5 percent. Your vote matters! The amount of people of color who stayed home and didn't exercise their right to vote in that election MATTERED.

Don't get me wrong. I'm not placing blame squarely on nonvoters. The Democratic Party and many of its candidates have not done the best job of addressing the needs and concerns of the most marginalized. The Democratic Party is tone-deaf and, in my opinion, saturated with white people who could care less about the needs of Ray-Ray and Keisha on street corners across America. But nevertheless, Stacey Abrams should have been governor of Georgia. We are all indebted to her and other courageous Black women like LaTosha Brown of Black Voters Matter, DeJuana Thompson of Woke Vote, Helen Butler and Mary-Pat Hector of the Georgia Coalition for the Peoples' Agenda, who invested so much to ensure that our voices counted as a community. Georgia hadn't been a blue state since 1992.

That's twenty-eight years of tradition in a Southern state transformed because activists, celebrities, philanthropists, politicians, and everyday people united. Don't tell me your vote doesn't count. That is no longer an excuse to recuse yourself of the responsibility that the ancestors tasked you with, Black people. In the beginning of this book, I asked people to pick a side. Racist or anti-racist. Black people, you aren't exempt. You must choose too. Are you contributing to equality or detracting from it? If you are a nonvoter, you are cancerous to the movement too; when we let up, we lose. Our opponents haven't rested for 400 years and won't start now. The movement is progressive. We may not get everything we want at one time from one candidate, but if we chip away at the goal, little by little, the small wins will add up. We don't need a perfect president, or governor, or school board president, or mayor.

We need leaders who align with freedom as closely as possible. We need leaders who respect the power of our votes.

This is a marathon movement, not a sprint. We must pace ourselves for the journey and make things a little better for each generation who comes after us.

FREEDOM OR ELSE

In 2021, when progressives have a powerful influence over the White House and the entire federal government, there should be no excuse for not obtaining some of the things we've been fighting for, as long as we all realize that we still will have to fight. We must build the America we want to see, and when hope is fleeting, I look to my brothers and sisters in this freedom fight beside me. One of the most brilliant political minds of our generation is my brother and co-founder of Until Freedom, Angelo Pinto:

America needs to be raised up. And you only raise up two things, a thing that is either dead or a child. America will get to decide which truth will be its own. If it is wise enough to choose the latter, I don't have faith that Joe Biden or any privileged white man will know how to, let alone have the gumption, to raise her up. I do have faith in the places where faith, promise, and transformation have always risen from the ashes and resurrected themselves. My faith is in the Black boy in solitary confinement who chooses freedom over hate. Faith in the mother separated from her children at the border who has resolved in her mind that she will create a brighter tomorrow for her children. Faith in the Black organizers in the Deep South that turned a red state blue. Faith in families who have loved ones killed by police who pursue justice. Faith that the frontline protesters will KEEP GOING! Faith that my daughter will see a Black woman like Tamika Mallory leading a movement and know that freedom isn't simply possible, it's on the way. That not only must we do something for others—we must do something different for ourselves.

Will we be different? Progressives, will you do something? Black people, will you have faith in the power of our unity to move forward in the mission to raise a dying America? Seekers of freedom, allies and accomplices of marginalized communities, your collective choice to raise up this country is the only way we can eradicate the racism that infects American politics. Key word is "collective." "I" cannot do it alone. The burden cannot be placed on a single vote. The history of this country, the soiled legacy of bigotry and inequality, will demolish that singular effort, but to believe in our ability to rebirth and raise a new America one vote at a time, collectively, throwing away divisiveness planted by overseers who don't want us to unite . . . when we maintain that cohesiveness, the power of our ballot will be strong enough to change the world. So, yes, your vote matters because it strengthens mine.

APPLY PRESSURE

The presidential election occurs every four years, and we flock to those major political moments because so much advertising is done to gain the attention of our communities, but we often forget that smaller local politics are equally important. I would go as far to say that there is less advertising during those times because people don't want us to realize the power of the outcomes of the local elections. I've heard time and time again that Black people feel like it doesn't matter who is in office because they don't do anything for the Black community anyway. That sentiment is untrue. The issue is, you're looking at politics from a macro level. Big elections are for big problems. You may not be able to tell what changes are occurring, but trust that they are happening. Some of them are good for us and others are not.

This is why we must be engaged and keep our eyes on all the moving pieces. Black folks are so tired that too many of us have checked out of politics, but literally everything that affects the quality of your life is political. Local politics affect you at a micro level. That pothole on your street that keeps tearing up the front-wheel alignment on your car . . . local politics. The graffiti on the side of the school building is local politics. The trash tarnishing the parks where your kids play? Local politics. Everything is affected by politics. From gas prices, to sex, to our access to health care, to the water we drink. Hell, from the extensions we wear in our hair, to the clothes we purchase from our favorite clothing boutique, even these are political because they are controlled by international trade laws. If you want influence over these things, you have to get involved in politics. You must vote. You have to vote down ballot.

For those who don't know, let me break it down for you. "Down ballot" simply means vote in small local elections as well as the larger national races. Remember, even the presidential election has other races down the ballot that you must participate in. You can't fail to show up at the polls. We might as well get in the habit of voting in every election, all the time.

Take the time to arm yourself with research about the candidates before you walk into the booth, so that you are voting with intention for the candidate who best serves your community's needs.

Let's do away with voting for last names that sound familiar. Let's do away with voting down the Democratic line without knowing any of the candidates. Those bad habits have not worked. Research! Research! Research! Black people must become acquainted with politics the way we are acquainted with our culture, with our music, with our art. We need to learn politics the way we have learned the entrepreneurial space. There are a lot of new Black millionaires who climbed to wealth out of the mud. They built empires and established equity in the business industry through trial and error. First-generation entrepreneurs. We need to do the same in politics. We need to go after politics like we go after a dollar, because money without power is just paper. It's just paper when your children's schools are still failing. It's just paper when a mass shooter can walk into a store and purchase a gun without a mental health screening or background check.

Establishing a presence not just in the numbers headed to the booth but on the ballot is important. We have to run for office. We must stop relying on people outside our communities to represent our interests, and throw our hats in the race to represent our own. And we must support Black candidates. Political campaigns require financing, and Black candidates may not always have capital to take it all the way. Prioritizing candidates from our communities benefits us all. We have to reallocate the resources in our communities, deducting from the $1.3 trillion Black folks spend per year. An investment in leadership is vital to implementing real change. Stop saying politics isn't your thing. Stop saying it doesn't matter who sits in office.

Hopelessness is not the same thing as helplessness. I know that hope is scarce, especially after Trump has been in office. It was leadership that caused daily trauma. Communities of color have always mistrusted the big system because we have been mistreated and persecuted time and time again, but I watched the system work in the 2020 election. I watched Black people take up arms against corruption and injustice. I watched solidarity push people of color to the polls. Were we hopeless? In many ways, yes. Did we elect the perfect candidates? I don't believe so. The disenfranchised have been programmed to mistrust the institution, but there comes a day when you cannot just stand by. You cannot allow politics to take place without you. Ninety percent of Black women showed up to support the Biden/Harris ticket. Black women carried the responsibility of removing Donald Trump from office, and despite previous defeats, despite decades of tears crying over the murders of Black men, despite a racially tense climate, despite it feeling impossible, and against the odds of a deadly pandemic, we flooded the polls and we won. Over 80 percent of Black men showed up to support the Democratic ticket in the 2020 race. Black people decided that enough was enough, that tears produced no results, that being idle didn't guarantee safety, and we unified to make sure that our votes were impactful. Like always, we carried the rest of the country on our backs. Solidarity and the tenacity to believe in a biased democracy, to play the game and learn the rules of it, helped us circumvent suppression at the polls. We played the game of politics, engaging with expertise, and we were heard. Finally, we were counted. Not three-fifths but in unified and large proportions. Imagine if we showed up in our local elections in such solidarity. We have to get involved to evolve. The political agenda of the democracy has not changed because the players have not changed. We must hop off the porch and take it to the streets. It is not only our civic duty but our obligation to our ancestors. We are forever in their debt, and every time we vote, we pay homage to their legacy.

So, what's next? What comes after a tyrannous regime that inflamed tense race relations? Donald Trump rejuvenated an old sentiment of bigotry. He gave white supremacists a feeling of entitlement that has infected every part of how our communities interact. We don't trust one another. We have been operating out of fear because leadership spread an infection of hate that makes it hard to trust the intentions of people outside of your immediate community. Using our vote as a weapon of activism was only the first step.

We are not out of troubled waters just because Donald Trump is out of office. The state of emergency that we are in as Americans did not begin with the Trump administration, and it did not end with his eviction. The problems we face stem from the history of division that built our nation. We must actively go against divisive legislation, against programming that is noninclusive, against policy that puts resources and wealth out of reach for the people who need them the most. Every citizen who identifies as anti-racist must be intolerant of police brutality. Systems of oppression persist when the people allow them to. We cannot condone an America that murders innocent citizens. We go to war against foreign countries for violating human rights but allow Black people right here on our own soil to be brutalized.

President Biden and Vice President Harris had some serious work to do. A passing of the baton was never going to be enough. Now is not the time to take our feet off the gas. If racism were the doing of one man, it wouldn't have persisted for hundreds of years. The ideologies of an individual would die off with the ending of his term. Racism is a problem child of the institution. Although President Biden was the better candidate of the two, we can't allow ourselves to get comfortable. A new president is not enough.

We must be diligent in our pursuit for equity in this country. Representation and equality are important, but equity and justice are the goals. A focus on representation is being satisfied with having a Black president, a Black CEO, a Black doctor. It's the institution putting that one Black person in place that allows them to say, "See, we made room for one President Obama, one Beyoncé, one LeBron James, one seat, one spot, that Black folks fight over. When the goal is just representation, some will think that Vice President Kamala Harris' appointment is enough for us to pump the brakes on the revolution. It isn't enough. Pushing forward in the pursuit of an elevated station in society that demands respect and resources is what keeps us fighting no matter who holds office. Equity. Justice.

Equality says, "We allow it to be possible for one Black person to exist in this position."

Equity says, "Black people will take up as much space and claim as much ownership as any other race." We don't want one reserved token seat at the table. We want access to pull up a chair whenever we are qualified without being hindered. More important, we want access to resources to build our own table. Equity allows Black women to show up to the hospital and get the same treatment for women's health issues that white women get. Equity allows Black and brown children to receive the same quality education as white children. Equity allows Black citizens to qualify for home purchases in any community and also not to be denied funding to start businesses. We want a piece of the pie, a pie we helped to prepare but have been excluded from enjoying.

Justice and equity are the challenges we continue to face. There will be no winning in America until we reach those goals, and we are still far from both. Use your voice, cast your votes, and demand the change that vote represented. Politicians may drag their feet and play poli-tricks, but they also know their jobs depend on your vote. Now we need to understand that too.

Fifteen

The Fight Is Not Yet Won

WHERE DO WE GO FROM HERE?

New leadership is not an automatic fix for the state of disrepair we are in. This nation is torn apart. We're fighting a pandemic that will leave scars for generations. There are a lot of people suffering under the crushing weight of poverty. Too many Black and brown mothers burying their sons. Too many people without health care. Too many schools underfunded. Too many city blocks with more liquor stores than fresh grocery options. While there is some obvious relief for booting a racist from the White House, our fight has just begun. We haven't won anything yet. We have no equity in the country we built, so when I see people celebrating the results of this election, I can't help but feel that we are counting the chickens before the eggs hatch. I get a little nervous when we celebrate, but don't get me wrong, we do have to acknowledge important milestones.

Certainly, defeating Donald Trump was critical, but it is not total victory. President Biden isn't the win. He was the best choice of the candidates, but his election couldn't erase four hundred years of systemic injustice. The Biden/Harris ticket is a pathway that leads us toward change if and only if we apply pressure. The White House had been transformed into an unwelcoming and dangerous place. People are eager to feel the return of integrity and pride to our nation's capital. I remember what that felt like, to be proud to be invited to the White House, to be regaled by an administration that is representative of decency. I enjoyed that feeling for eight years under our forever leader, President Barack Obama, even though at times we challenged him and definitely should have pushed way more.

I remember my dear friend Michael Blake inviting me to attend a movie screening at the White House hosted by the beautiful first lady Michelle Obama. I was among less than twenty people who were granted access to screen the movie *The Help*. Moments under their care at 1600 Pennsylvania Avenue were some of the most memorable times of my career. I can recall crossing paths with Michelle Obama at other events and introducing myself every single time. I never wanted to assume that she remembered who I was. One day I introduced myself again and she said, "Yes, Tamika, I know who you are." It felt so good for her to know me and my work. So, I get it. The desire to have that again. The need to have leadership. Those were incredible moments for me, and we need those moments again, but it's too soon to be traipsing back for dinner parties and dancing in the streets of DC.

It would feel so good to be confident and comfortable with the leadership that I can let my guard down, but that is not where we are in this moment. I must find purpose and comfort being on the outside and being the one they don't want to see coming. I'm prepared to hold the line outside the White House and shake the trees until we watch the leaves of injustice fall from the limbs of an archaic institution. Since Black and brown voters are always asked to help secure the White House, those who want to stay there must attend to the political and social needs of our community. We now have leverage. Justice and equity are the goals.

Don't mistake my anger over these issues as a closed door. I welcome conversations with the new administration, and I welcome the support of other communities. We need our allies and accomplices to fight this battle against racist patriarchal institutions. It is only solidarity that leads to progression. I don't want to box you out if you're from a neighboring community. I want to embrace you. I want to stand by you as long as you're willing to stand up for me and people who look like me when we're in the thick of it. If you're ready to handle the inconvenient and unfair consequences that come with chasing justice.

Unified, we are powerful enough to push the priority of our issues to Vice President Harris. I name her because she, more than President Biden, was responsible for my vote. I have no desire to try to discern whether racist ideologies of the past may still exist within our 45th president. He was proxy to

Vice President Kamala Harris, a Black woman, whose values aligned most closely with my own. I'm sure many Americans could see a portion of their reflection when looking at her life. She represents so many different communities and is representative of everything American, because before we were known as the country that elected Donald Trump, we were known as a melting pot of different communities. She is as American as it gets. She is relatable to the communities we seek to deliver justice for. During the election season, we talked a lot about Kamala Harris's time as a prosecutor, but I am conscious of the era she was in. Vice President Harris operated within a system that criminalized Black people for sport. And her job was to prosecute criminals. She was a minority woman in a white, male-dominated field that is built on oppression. I wish she had been a revolutionary. But now we are in a new time. All I can do is pray she's ready to live up to the challenge set before her. I can only hope she will be overwhelmed with a revolutionary spirit.

I voted for Kamala Harris's promise in the hope that she will live up to it and not fall privy to the tradition of bigotry and institutional oppression of its own citizens. Just her picture in the history books, next to generation after generation of white men, is historic. Just her nomination undermines white supremacy. I hope her policy and her power are rooted in the courage to go against that as well, making room to heal the broken communities that have suffered far too long.

This moment calls for us to go harder, to organize. To think critically about things that we were told are just the way they are, like the electoral college, the Supreme Court, and the criminal-legal system. We also need to continue to push for a sustainable environment, health care for all, funded public education, safe housing for everyone, and an economic system that is rooted in people, not profit, because capitalism has created a society of unnecessary suffering. Excuse me for my colloquialisms, but we must keep our foot on the neck of the powers that be. We will not blindly follow party loyalty. They must earn their reelection, so now is the time to call for the change this country so desperately needs. If they want our vote, we want legislation that begins to repair the damage that has been done to Black and brown communities since this country's founding.

So a celebration is not called for until this new administration lives up to the promises that were made during the campaign, but not only those promises—they must live up to our expectations. There is no quick fix for the political disgrace that Donald Trump made of our country. President Biden and Vice President Harris have their work cut out for them. They are still operating within a system that is corrupt. It is rotten. They must turn over the soil in order to grow a new political landscape for us all. It will take time to repair both the nation's reputation and the four hundred plus years of oppression of the Black community who built this country with our bare hands. While the global image will take some time to repair, we will not sit idly.

We will not move along as novice political puppets who are called upon only when it is time to be counted. We will fight to win the country we built. I was always taught that closed mouths don't get fed, so during these next four years, I'm not waiting for President Biden and Vice President Harris to tell me what's on the menu. I'm going to open my mouth and speak up to tell them what my community needs to be served.

POLITICAL POWER

Minority communities and allies of these communities, specifically Black and brown communities, must build a formal entity that represents the interests of the people. We must educate ourselves on the political process, educate our children on the political process, and form a coalition that the democracy recognizes as the key to unlocking the votes in our communities. Solidarity brings strength to our voices. If we are represented under one faction, we can collect a list of needs, put in place a board of politicians and leaders who can express those needs, and create the demands that must be satisfied before we give our collective votes to any political party. Many have tried to form their own party, a Black or brown political party, but we aren't ready for that. Doing that will only split the Black vote and decrease our power even further. We need a union of sorts that unites us in a political way that increases our power. This needs to be developed over the next four years, organizing in a way that makes our voices more potent. Once we outline our agenda, the leaders of this political organization will present them to the administration for support. Only when our community's issues are made a priority of the candidates will we endorse one and deliver a collective minority vote. Building this is the challenge and takes true leadership and committed grassroots efforts to educate and organize our political power.

This is what we need on the table:

1. Reform criminal justice

- Immediate elimination of qualified immunity. A police officer cannot be sued through personal litigation. We are no longer willing to allow the protection of violent cops. Officers who brutalize people of color must be charged with a hate crime and should not be protected from personal liability for constitutional violations.

- Reallocation of resources and reimagining the type of support that is dispatched for emergency calls: Not every circumstance requires a police officer's presence. Most need mental health experts, community liaisons and representatives, and members of community resource programs who have been designed and trained to respond to nonviolent issues in the community. The implementation of crisis management systems,[1] like the one New York City has leaned on to decrease violent crime, must be formed in every major city where violence impacts quality of life. New York has seen a 40 percent decrease in shootings since 2010. They are doing something right.

There is something to be learned from their efforts that can save Black lives across America. Violence interruption teams in Baltimore[2] and elsewhere across the country have proved to be effective, even though they operate on shoestring budgets. We need to fully fund these nonpolice alternative approaches to public safety and others. The BREATHE Act from the Movement for Black Lives presents a new vision for public safety and outlines how to divest from systems of punishment and invest in our communities at the federal and state levels.[3]

- The development of transformative alternatives to incarceration that are not rooted in punishment and control but in accountability and care. Transformative justice is a framework that can guide alternatives so we can end cycles of harm and build safe and accountable communities.

2. Economic justice

- There needs to be an increase in minimum wage. We also need improved public housing that is protected under legislation that prevents it from being gentrified by entities and individuals outside of the community. There is also a need for a universal guaranteed income to abolish poverty,[4] as championed by Rev. Dr. Martin Luther King, Jr., when in 1967 he wrote,[5] "I am now convinced that the solution to poverty is to abolish it directly by a now widely discussed measure: the guaranteed income."

3. Education

- This country's wealth was built on the backs of our ancestors who were deprived of the basic rights of reading and writing. They paid the price of our education in blood. Black students who desire to attend a public two- or four-year institution should be able to do so for free, and student housing and course materials, including books, should be covered under a federally funded grant system. Cancel student debt NOW. And ensure schools in Black and brown communities have the resources they need to thrive.

4. Reparations

- In order to heal, we must stop the bleeding of the wound. The Black community has suffered under America's racist history long enough. We are owed, deserve, and are entitled to reparations for the crimes committed against humanity over the course of this country's existence. History can't be erased, but we can close the book. This administration can represent the writing of new pages while we unite as a country and recover from the tragic undermining that has taken place over these past four years under Donald Trump. Politicians have a way of gaslighting the Black community. You spin our history to us in a way that manipulates us into thinking it's ancient. You record it in ways that makes enslavement seem voluntary or humane. It was barbaric and torturous. It was an act motivated by hate, economics, and a sadistic need for an entire race of people to feel inferior. The Biden/ Harris administration immediately made history by changing the optics of what a vice president should look like. I'm calling for more than an optics switch. I'm calling for righteousness and justice to finally be served to a community of people, my community, the Black community, who has never quite recovered from the free labor that our ancestors were forced to give. Empower us with finances that can lift us out of poverty. Begin the first page of a new history for America. Write into history the repentance and the unity of two communities that have historically been separated. Wash away the bad blood and birth a new national sentiment that equality and freedom are more than things to be sung about in a national anthem or written about in a constitution that isn't inclusive. Answer the call I am putting out for my community. It's dire. It's emergent. It cannot wait. End the state of emergency that Black people have been living in. Land of the free, home of the brave. Be brave enough to be the first to truly stand on that. To truly give freedom to all people. Political freedom, educational freedom, financial freedom. Compensate our pain. Let us roam free, let us live free, without the fear of being hunted by the institution that sees our skin as a target.

And damn it . . . arrest the cops, charge the cops . . .

Until Freedom.
Until Freedom.
Until Freedom.

Until freedom is reached, I will not stop. We will not stop. We cannot stop. I am ringing the alarms because we are in trouble. We are in a state of emergency until Freedom.

I'm tired of talking, tired of my tears being transformed to sound bites every time another Black child of God is turned into a trophy of this racist system. I'm done talking. It's action time. We can tear it down or build it up together. What will you do, President Biden? What will you do, Vice President Harris? What will each of us do? Respectfully . . . do something!

And the final rule for my people:

Rule #15: Be unapologetic about your Blackness until they respect it. Until Freedom.

Sincerely,
Tamika D. Mallory
I'm out.

Acknowledgments

This book had so many hands that helped feed her. I am grateful beyond measure to a vast group of people whose belief in me is invaluable.

I need to start with two Black women, Latoya Bond, my manager, and Ashley Antoinette Coleman, my literary agent. These audacious, dedicated, amazing women remind me that the support of other Black women can make anything happen. I am writing these words today because of their selfless dedication to this collective dream called "State of Emergency."

My gratitude will never be enough for my Until Freedom family: Linda Sarsour, Angelo Pinto, Mysonne Linen, and all of our extended loved ones. They believe in me more than I believe in myself. And with that belief, they titled me their leader—the highest honor, from the greatest leaders of a generation. When I was at the lowest point of my life, when I saw no value in myself and the world had beat me down, my brothers and sister picked me up, dusted me off, and put me back together. The vulnerability we share with each other calls us to our highest selves. God put this family together. Man shall not tear us apart. I am forever indebted to each of you. Thank you!

My family is like no other—they are my rocks, my cheerleaders, my team. I love you all so much. To all my aunts and uncles; my cousins; my brother, Milton; my sister Dana; my bro-cousin Derrick; and my god sister, Nadine; my nieces and great nephews; and to Don Coleman, I am so grateful for each one of you. You all put joy in my heart with every encounter.

To my sister Sharon and niece Skylar, thank you for being my steady homegirls, and for bearing the weight of mom's care.

To my heartbeat, my son, Tarique Ryans, you know the vibes.

Daddy, you are my number-one guy—the days of my childhood when you would force me to go to rallies and marches, I thought you were punishing me. Instead, I now know you were setting me up for my future and giving me keen insight into the Black experience. I was paying attention. And Dad, you make it hard for me because if it ain't love like you love us and especially Mommy, I don't want it!

Mom—your strength and tenacity have literally shaped me as a woman, as a Black woman. My morals and standards, my heart, my love for our people, all comes from every fiber of your being. Along this journey you and Dad could have given up on me so many times, but you never did. I'm only a leader because of what I learned from you. You're the baddest chick alive!

To all of my friends, led by the captain, Jaime Perrington—it would be impossible to list you all. Some people say you only have a few real friends. Well that is not my story. I have tremendous and deep friendships. You all impact my life every day and make me strong and better. I cherish you individually and as my collective village.

To my team at Black Privilege Publishing and Simon & Schuster, my editor Nicholas Ciani and the rest of the team, thank you all for your time and energy, and for being such a solid and reliable sounding board for my nerves, my excitement, and my ideas. Thank you, Philip McHarris, for ensuring that I stated facts not fiction.

Thank you Rachel Noerdlinger, Marvet Britto, Monique Idlett, Hazel Dukes, Cora Masters Barry, Melanie Campbell, Erica Ford, Yandy Smith-Harris, Karen Boykin Towns, and Lu-Shawn Thompson for your sisterhood and mentorship.

Thank you to Marc Gerald of Europa Content for your belief in me. Thank you to Mark Thompson, Roland S. Martin, and A. T. Mitchell for your friendship and support.

I am honored and still in awe that two legends, Angela Y. Davis and Cardi B, contributed to the foreword of this book.

Thank you, Cardi B, for understanding the power of influence and using yours to push the movement forward. I count you as a friend.

To Angela Y. Davis, it is deeply meaningful to have a woman who fights so hard for our people give her time and words to me, and I hope I make you proud.

Charlamagne. Thank you, my brother, for your belief in me, your dedication, and your friendship. This has been some ride, and I am grateful to you for bringing me along on your journey.

While I have acknowledged everyone, I reserve my highest praise for God . . .

—TAMIKA

Notes

CHAPTER ONE: OUR MOMENT

1. Ibram X. Kendi, *How to Be an Antiracist* (New York: Random House Publishing Group, 2019).

CHAPTER TWO: LEGACY OF AN ACTIVIST

1. https://www.nytimes.com/2011/04/03/magazine/mag-03CivilWar-t .html?pagewanted=all&fbclid=IwAR2txkFKF_FjQhagG9 -hx2XufOs6Yh3kyzAKE9kXO_4ypDSmMAuHEly50tI.

2. Jim Miller, "Robert Mallory in the United States House of Representatives, July 5, 1862," *Civil War Notebook*, October 2, 2017, https://civilwarnotebook.blogspot.com/2017/10/robert-mallory-in -united-states-house.html.

3. Child Welfare Information Gateway (2020), "Foster Care Statistics 2018," Washington, DC: U.S. Department of Health and Human Services, Administration for Children and Families, Children's Bureau.

4. U.S. Census Bureau, "America's Families and Living Arrangements: 2019," The United States Census Bureau, accessed December 2, 2020, https://www.census.gov/data/tables/2019/demo/families/cps-2019.html.

5. Charles M. Blow, "Dads Are Doing Best of All," *The New York Times,* June 8, 2015, https://www.nytimes.com/2015/06/08/opinion/charles -blow-black-dads-are-doing-the-best-of-all.html.

6. Kirk E. Harris, "Low-Income Black Fathers Want to Be Good Dads: The System Won't Let Them," *The Guardian,* June 17, 2018, http://www .theguardian.com/commentisfree/2018/jun/17/black-fathers-parenting -child-support-policy-flaws.

7. Stephanie Brown, et al., "African American Extended Families and Kinship Care: How Relevant Is the Foster Care Model for Kinship Care?" *Children and Youth Services Review,* vol. 24, no. 1 (Jan. 2002): pp. 53–77, doi:10.1016/S0190-7409(01)00168-2.

CHAPTER FOUR: THE RULES

1. Henry Louis Gates, Jr., Originally posted on *The Root,* "How Many Slaves Landed in the U.S.? | The African Americans: Many Rivers to Cross | PBS," The African Americans: Many Rivers to Cross, January 2, 2013, https://www.pbs.org/wnet/african-americans-many -rivers-to-cross/history/how-many-slaves-landed-in-the-us/.

CHAPTER FIVE: THE U.S. VS. BLACK AMERICA

1. Gerald F. Goodwin, "Black and White in Vietnam," *The New York Times,* July 18, 2017, https://www.nytimes.com/2017/07/18/opinion /racism-vietnam-war.html.

2. "Vietnam War U.S. Military Fatal Casualty Statistics," National Archives, August 15, 2016, https://www.archives.gov/research/military /vietnam-war/casualty-statistics.

3. Donnie Summerlin, "Samuel Younge Jr." *Encyclopedia of Alabama,* accessed December 2, 2020, http://encyclopediaofalabama.org/article /h-1669.

4. Dan Baum, https://harpers.org/archive/2016/04/legalize-it-all.

5. Craig Delaval, https://www.pbs.org/wgbh/pages/frontline/shows/drugs /special/cia.html.

6. Gary Webb, *Dark Alliance: The CIA, the Contras, and the Crack Cocaine Explosion* (New York, London: Seven Stories Press, Turnaround, 1999).

7. Roland G. Fryer, et al., "Measuring Crack Cocaine and Its Impact," *Economic Inquiry* vol. 51, no. 3, Western Economic Association International (July 2013): p. 1651.

8. Text—H.R.3355—103rd Congress (1993–1994): Violent Crime Control and Law Enforcement Act of 1994 | Congress.Gov | Library of Congress, accessed December 2, 2020, https://www.congress.gov/bill /103rd-congress/house-bill/3355/text.

9. Carrie Johnson, "20 Years Later, Parts of Major Crime Bill Viewed as Terrible Mistake," NPR.org, September 12, 2014, https://www.npr.org /2014/09/12/347736999/20-years-later-major-crime-bill-viewed-as -terrible-mistake.

10. Alma Carten, "How Racism Has Shaped Welfare Policy in America since 1935," AP News, August 21, 2016, https://apnews.com/article /fbd5d3c83e3243e9b03e46d7cb842eaa.

11. Ife Floyd, "The Truth About 'Welfare Reform': TANF Is Disappearing," Center on Budget and Policy Priorities, December 12, 2017, https://www.cbpp.org/blog/the-truth-about -welfare-reform-tanf-is-disappearing-0.

CHAPTER SIX: THE ROOTS OF REBELLION

1. "Who Was Ella Baker?" Ella Baker Center for Human Rights, accessed December 2, 2020, https://ellabakercenter.org/who-was-ella-baker.

2. Barbara Ransby, "Ella Baker's Legacy Runs Deep: Know Her Name," *The New York Times,* January 20, 2020, NYTimes.com, https://www.nytimes.com/2020/01/20/opinion/martin-luther-king -ella-baker.html.

3. "Ella Baker: Biography & Facts," *Encyclopedia Britannica,* accessed December 2, 2020, https://www.britannica.com/biography/Ella-Baker.

CHAPTER SEVEN: SAY ALL THEIR NAMES

1. Richard Pérez-Peña, "Woman Tied to 1955 Emmett Till Murder Tells Historian Her Claims Were False," *The New York Times*, January 29, 2017.

CHAPTER EIGHT: NO WAY OUT

1. Becky Little, "Why Martin Luther King's Family Believes James Earl Ray Was Not His Killer," HISTORY, accessed December 2, 2020, https://www.history.com/news/who-killed-martin-luther-king-james -earl-ray-mlk-assassination.

2. Editors, History.com, "Malcolm X," HISTORY, accessed December 2, 2020, https://www.history.com/topics/black-history/malcolm-x.

3. Editors, History.com, "Black Panthers," HISTORY, accessed December 2, 2020, https://www.history.com/topics/civil-rights -movement/black-panthers.

4. Jessica Glenza, "Rosewood Massacre a Harrowing Tale of Racism and the Road Toward Reparations," *The Guardian,* January 3, 2016, http:// www.theguardian.com/us-news/2016/jan/03/rosewood-florida -massacre-racial-violence-reparations.

5. Alexis Clark, "Tulsa's 'Black Wall Street' Flourished as a Self- Contained Hub in Early 1900s," HISTORY September 4, 2019, https://www.history.com/news/black-wall-street-tulsa-race-massacre.

6. Pete Earley, "The Untold Story of One of America's Worst Race Riots," *The Washington Post*, September 12, 1982, https://www.washingtonpost .com/archive/opinions/1982/09/12/the-untold-story-of-one-of-americas -worst-race-riots/e37fc963-71dd-45cc-8cb0-04ab8032bcd2.

7. Alexis Clark, "Tulsa's 'Black Wall Street' Flourished as a Self-Contained Hub in Early 1900s," HISTORY, accessed December 2, 2020, https://www.history.com/news/black-wall-street-tulsa-race -massacre.

8. Nan Elizabeth Woodruff, "The Forgotten History of America's Worst Racial Massacre," *The New York Times,* September 30, 2019, NYTimes .com, https://www.nytimes.com/2019/09/30/opinion/elaine-massacre -1919-arkansas.html.

9. Ed Pilkington, "The Day Police Bombed a City Street: Can Scars of 1985 Move Atrocity Be Healed?" *The Guardian*, May 10, 2020, https:// www.theguardian.com/us-news/2020/may/10/move-1985-bombing -reconciliation-philadelphia.

10. Philip Bump, "This Is What the Average American Looks like in 2018," *The Washington Post*, August 13, 2018, https://www.washingtonpost .com/news/politics/wp/2018/08/13/this-is-what-the-average-american -looks-like-in-2018.

CHAPTER NINE: DEFUND THE POLICE

1. Ryan Felton, "Fixing Flint's Contaminated Water System Could Cost $216m, Report Says," *The Guardian,* June 6, 2016, http://www .theguardian.com/us-news/2016/jun/06/flint-water-crisis-lead-pipes -infrastructure-cost.

2. Marc Kilmer, "How Much Money Will Be Enough for Baltimore Schools?" Maryland Public Policy Institute, October 22, 2019, http:// www.mdpolicy.org/policyblog/detail/how-much-money-will-be-enough -for-baltimore-schools.

3. Philip V. McHarris, and Zellie Imani, "It Is Time to Cancel Student Debt and Make Higher Education Free," April 26, 2020, https://www .aljazeera.com/opinions/2020/4/26/it-is-time-to-cancel-student-debt -and-make-higher-education-free.

4. Philip V. McHarris, "Democrats Are Ignoring a Key Piece of Criminal Justice Reform—Slicing Police Budgets," *The Washington Post,* January 16, 2020, https://www.washingtonpost.com/outlook/2020/01/16

/democrats-are-ignoring-key-piece-criminal-justice-reform-slicing
-police-budgets.

5. Police Officers | Data USA, accessed January 27, 2021, https://datausa
.io/profile/soc/police-officers.

6. Bree Newsome Bass, "Black Cops Don't Make Policing Any Less Anti-
Black," *Medium,* October 22, 2020, https://level.medium.com/Black
-cops-dont-make-policing-any-less-anti-Black-4baf78c2ab29.

7. Conor Friedersdorf, "Police Have a Much Bigger Domestic-Abuse
Problem Than the NFL Does," *The Atlantic,* September 19, 2014,
https://www.theatlantic.com/national/archive/2014/09/police-officers
-who-hit-their-wives-or-girlfriends/380329.

8. Ejeris Dixon, and Leah Lakshmi Piepzna-Samarasinha, editors,
*Beyond Survival: Strategies and Stories from the Transformative Justice
Movement,* Annotated edition (Chico, CA: AK Press, 2020).

9. Movement for Black Lives, The Breathe Act, 2020, https://breatheact.org.

10. Philip V. McHarris and Thenjiwe McHarris, "No More Money for the
Police," *The New York Times,* May 30, 2020, https://www.nytimes.com
/2020/05/30/opinion/george-floyd-police-funding.html.

11. Kimberlé Crenshaw, et al., *Say Her Name: Resisting Police Brutality
Against Black Women*, (New York: African American Policy Forum,
2015).

CHAPTER TEN: HARNESSING THE POWER OF OUR VOICE

1. Jacob Passy, "Black Homeownership Has Declined Since 2012—
Here's Where Black Households Are Most Likely to Be Homeowners,"
MarketWatch, July 1, 2020, https://www.marketwatch.com/story
/Black-homeownership-has-declined-since-2012-heres-where-Black
-households-are-most-likely-to-be-homeowners-2020-06-30.

2. Editors, History.com, "Greensboro Sit-In," HISTORY, accessed
December 2, 2020, https://www.history.com/topics/Black-history
/the-greensboro-sit-in.

CHAPTER ELEVEN: OTHER STRATEGIES FOR CHANGE

1. Stanford University, "Montgomery Bus Boycott," The Martin Luther
King, Jr., Research and Education Institute, April 26, 2017, https://
kinginstitute.stanford.edu/encyclopedia/montgomery-bus-boycott.

2. Bruce C.T. Wright, "Black Buying Power by the Numbers: History in the Making," NewsOne, February 10, 2020, https://newsone.com /3901998/Black-buying-power-by-numbers-history-making.

3. Richard Pérez-Peña, "Woman Tied to 1955 Emmett Till Murder Tells Historian Her Claims Were False," *The New York Times*, January 29, 2017.

4. Jerry Mitchell, "Bombshell Quote Missing from Emmett Till Tape. So Did Carolyn Bryant Donham Really Recant?" *Clarion Ledger*, August 21, 2018, https://www.clarionledger.com/story/news/2018/08/21/emmett -till-carolyn-bryant-donham-recant-quote-missing/1017876002.

CHAPTER THIRTEEN: CANNOT STAND

1. Henry Louis Gates, Jr., "How Many Slaves Landed in the U.S.? | The African Americans: Many Rivers to Cross | PBS," Originally posted on *The Root,* January 2, 2013, https://www.pbs.org/wnet /african-americans-many-rivers-to-cross/history/how-many-slaves -landed-in-the-us/.

CHAPTER FOURTEEN: VOTE AND BUILD

1. Essence, "55 Percent of White Women, 18 Percent of Black Men Voted for Donald Trump: Exit Poll," *Essence,* November 4, 2020, https:// www.essence.com/news/politics/55-percent-White-women-trump -election-2020.

2. Stanford University, "Jackson, Jimmie Lee," The Martin Luther King, Jr., Research and Education Institute, June 22, 2017, https:// kinginstitute.stanford.edu/encyclopedia/jackson-jimmie-lee.

CHAPTER FIFTEEN: THE FIGHT IS NOT YET WON

1. City of New York, Crisis Management System, accessed December 7, 2020, https://www1.nyc.gov/site/peacenyc/interventions/crisis -management.page.

2. Daniel W. Webster, Jennifer Mendel Whitehill, Jon S. Vernick, and Elizabeth M. Parker, "Evaluation of Baltimore's Safe Streets Program: Effects on Attitudes, Participants' Experiences, and Gun Violence," 2012, Johns Hopkins Bloomberg School of Public Health.

3. Movement for Black Lives, The Breathe Act, 2020, https://breathe act.org.

4. Aja Brown, "King's Dream of Guaranteed Income Is Long Past Overdue," *The Hill*, January 17, 2021, https://thehill.com/opinion/civil-rights/534556-kings-dream-of-guaranteed-income-is-long-past-overdue.

5. Martin Luther King, Jr., *Where Do We Go from Here: Chaos or Community?* (New York: Harper & Row, 1967).

Index

About the Author

Tamika D. Mallory is a trailblazing social justice leader, movement strategist, globally recognized civil rights activist, and cofounder of Until Freedom and the historic Women's March. She served as the youngest-ever executive director of the National Action Network. Her speech in the wake of the murder of George Floyd in Minneapolis, Minnesota—entitled "State of Emergency"—was dubbed "the speech of a generation" by ABC News. Mallory is an expert in the areas of gun violence prevention, women's rights, criminal justice reform, and grassroots organizing.

Tamika's firm, Mallory Consulting, is a strategic planning and event management corporation that works with Fortune 500 corporations and organizations on flagship projects related to mass incarceration, gun violence, and police brutality.

Tamika's honors include being named to the 2017 *Time* 100 Pioneers List, and *Fortune*'s 2017 list of the World's Greatest Leaders, winning a 2017 BET Shine a Light award, and a nomination for the Social Justice Impact award at the 2021 NAACP Image Awards.